EXPLORING
GRAMERCY PARK
— AND —
UNION SQUARE

EXPLORING
GRAMERCY PARK

--- A N D ---

UNION SQUARE

ALFRED POMMER & JOYCE POMMER

THE
History
PRESS

Published by The History Press
Charleston, SC
www.historypress.net

Front cover: Original paintings by Ann Woodward.
Back cover: Union Square, George Washington. Courtesy Library of Congress,
Prints and Photographs Division, Record # LC-DIG- det-4aa 08050.

Unless otherwise noted, all images appear courtesy of Alfred Pommer.

First published 2015

Manufactured in the United States

ISBN 978.1.62619.854.8

Library of Congress Control Number: 2015947681

Notice: The information in this book is true and complete to the best of our
knowledge. It is offered without guarantee on the part of the author or The
History Press. The author and The History Press disclaim all liability in
connection with the use of this book.

DISCARDED

CONTENTS

CONTENTS

ACKNOWLEDGEMENTS

The authors would like to thank our commissioning agent Whitney Landis for her expertise, flexibility and generous spirit, which made working with her a pleasure. And much recognition must also go to the talented and accomplished Ann Woodward for her long hours of hard work in creating the exquisite drawings and paintings that enhance this book, along with its front cover.

The authors would also like to acknowledge our debt to the *AIA Guide of New York*, the *Guide to New York City Landmarks* (New York City Landmarks Preservation Commission), the Art Commission and the *Municipal Art Society Guide to Manhattan's Outdoor Sculpture* and to the many other books, especially those listed in the bibliography, that contributed to making our guide book possible.

INTRODUCTION

This is a unique guidebook because I will guide you each step of the way so you can walk through all or part of the neighborhoods at your leisure—or you can enjoy the guidebook, with its variety of descriptions, illustrations and photographs from a comfortable chair. My armchair guidebook takes you on a walk through the Gramercy Park Historic District and a bit of its surrounding neighborhood. We will explore the neighborhood's history and some interesting stories, along with its architecture (including homes of wealthy New Yorkers that are now over 150 years old—a mansion and several townhouses, along with modern and postmodern buildings in the neighborhood).

Gramercy Park was one of Manhattan's Four Squares (Union Square, Madison Square, Stuyvesant Square and Gramercy Square), four wealthy residential neighborhoods developed by Samuel Ruggles between 1830 and 1850. They were created as residential squares, with a park surrounded by homes of rich New Yorkers. After the Civil War, Union Square, Madison Square and Stuyvesant Square were losing their prosperous residents as pressures from commercialization and immigration increased and well-to-do New Yorkers were moving northward into Murray Hill and farther north along Fifth Avenue and, as the Gilded Age came about, into what became known as Millionaires' Mile along Fifth Avenue between East Sixtieth Street and East Ninety-sixth Street.

Throughout all this and during the twentieth century right up to the present, Gramercy Park continued as an affluent neighborhood and never

Gramercy Park historic plaque at Gramercy Park's Irving Place entrance.

experienced the changing fortunes the other three neighborhoods did. The difference between Gramercy and the other neighborhoods may well stem from the event that occurred on December 13, 1831, when Ruggles legally established that the land (forty-two lots, about two acres) at the center of his Gramercy plot was to be deeded to the people who purchased the surrounding sixty-six lots. Ruggles provided that five trustees be placed in charge of the park's design and maintenance. The trustees were to be replaced when needed by neighborhood elections. This arrangement was quite different from that of the other three neighborhoods where the land in the center, which Ruggles designated for a park, was donated (for one or five dollars) to the city with an agreement that the city build and maintain a park for the neighborhood. The immediate effect of this did increase the value of the surrounding lots, but in the long run, Gramercy Park survived better as an affluent neighborhood with its private park, owned and maintained by the surrounding landowners.

Each of the city's many neighborhoods differ in any number of ways, but they all share the vitality and creative drive that makes New York City special. While many of the other Manhattan neighborhoods were represented by struggling artists, striving entrepreneurs, wealthy enclaves, a developing middle class, a struggling working class or somewhat of a mix of the aforementioned, Gramercy developed over its first one hundred years as a concentrated unique mix of well-to-do New Yorkers who promoted a community atmosphere of interacting and shared purpose that allowed Gramercy to become so much more than just a private park surrounded by mansions. The environment was special in the way it attracted and nourished an amazing number of talented people, who were motivated, productive and decent, to work and live together within the bounds of its neighborhood.

Over time, the cast of important people changed, but right from its inception, the park was inspired by two noteworthy but for the most part forgotten men: Samuel Ruggles, the visionary who created Manhattan's Four Squares and lived on Union Square, and his son-in-law, George Templeton Strong, who lived on Gramercy Square and may well be considered a moral compass for his neighborhood. Later came James Harper, Dr. Valentine Mott, Edwin Booth, Stanford White, John Barrymore Jr., George Bellows, Robert Henri, Ida Tarbell, Elsie de Wolfe, Nathanael West, O. Henry, Samuel Tilden, Theda Bara, Norman Thomas, Thomas Edison, Emma Thursby, John Carradine, Margaret Hamilton and Jimmy Cagney, all living, at different points in time, within a block of one another. There were so many more, including Teddy Roosevelt, Carl Van Vechten, Robert Winthrop Chanler, Ted Husing, Mrs. Patrick Campbell, George Wolfe, Lincoln Kirstein, Louise Bourgeois, Elinor and William Rose Benet—and let's not forget Calvert Vaux, Briton Hadden and Henry Luce.

As we walk through the Gramercy Park neighborhood, I'll talk about the famous and infamous and point out the various locations where the talented artists, writers, actors and politicians have lived and worked. You may be surprised that such a wide and diverse collection of innovative and talented individuals lived and worked in one relatively small neighborhood. For over one hundred years, the unchanging nature of this small exceptional neighborhood nurtured a creative drive that it held in common with the rest of the city's widespread neighborhoods—the drive and vitality that makes this city special.

We will pass the site where O. Henry lived, where he drank and where he wrote "The Gift of the Magi." You will find out about the "bachelors" and their motto: "never complain, never explain." You will see the house where Elinor Wylie died and the house where Lincoln Kirstein lived for fifty years and where George Wolfe lives now. We will pass the church where Eleanor Roosevelt was baptized.

You will get the answer to questions such as: Who was "the Vamp" who lived on "Block Beautiful"? Why are there two doorways with giraffes?

INTRODUCTION

Where did the "wicked witch of the west" live? Who was the Socialist who lived most of his life on Gramercy Park and ran for president of the United States six times? Who donated his mansion to the "Players Club" so that actors could mingle with "normal" people? What was Samuel Tilden afraid of? Why was Dr. Valentine Mott so hated in some circles and honored in others? What is George Templeton Strong remembered for? Who was the meanest man in New York City? Who was the famous New Yorker who said, "Too many good women were tied to no-good men simply because they lacked the means to make a living" and what did he do about it?

You will find out about the literary murder of the century in 1910, as well as the many more interesting people who are covered in this guidebook. And I am hoping that by taking this journey through Gramercy Park's past together, we might get an idea of what it was that made this very small part of Manhattan special.

When I use the phrase "New York City landmark," it means that the structure is designated by the New York City Landmarks Preservation Commission as an official New York City landmark. When I state that a structure is a "national landmark," I am saying that the structure is listed on the National Register of Historic Places. Some buildings and historic districts (Gramercy Park) are both.

Roughly speaking, the boundaries for the Gramercy Park neighborhood go from East Twenty-third Street to East Seventeenth Street and from Park Avenue South to Third Avenue.

The boundaries for the New York City Gramercy Park Historic District, designated in 1966, and its extension, designated in 1988, are more explicit and include: Gramercy Park West and East Twenty-first Street (Gramercy Park North) to Gramercy Park East to East Eighteenth Street and East Nineteenth Street between Third Avenue and Irving Place. It includes one building (nos. 119–121) on East Eighteenth Street between Irving Place and Park Avenue South. It also includes a good part of Gramercy Park South (East Twentieth Street) between Third Avenue and Park Avenue South; Calvary Church on the northeast corner of Gramercy Park East/East Twenty-first Street and a small part of Park Avenue South is also in the historic district.

There is a proposed new extension for this historic district that includes additional buildings on the west side of Third Avenue between East Eighteenth and East Twenty-second Streets, as well as 40, 44, 45 and 60 Gramercy Park North.

Also on East Twenty-second Street and included in the proposed new extension are the United Charities Building, Manhattan Trade School for

Girls, Gramercy Arms, Sage House (on Lexington Avenue), Family Court Building, Gramercy Court, Miss E.L. Breese Carriage House and Gustavus Adolphus Swedish Lutheran Church, and possibly a few more buildings may be included.

On East Nineteenth Street, between Irving Place and Park Avenue South, the expansion would include the old IRT Co. Substation building, and several additional buildings are being considered, along with 65, 67 and 71 Irving Place.

One block south of the Gramercy Park Historic District, we find East Seventeenth Street between Third Avenue and Park Avenue South, a two-block area that is included in this walking tour because of some interesting buildings and stories that are part of Gramercy neighborhood's history. Part of this area includes the East Seventeenth Street Irving Place Historic District, which runs from 47 and 49 Irving Place and 122 East Seventeenth Street to 104 East Seventeenth Street (on the south side of East Seventeenth Street).

The boundaries for the national Gramercy Park historic district are from Third Avenue to Park Avenue South and East Eighteenth Street to East Twenty-second Street.

Chapter 1

LOCAL HISTORY

During the colonial era, the land that makes up today's Gramercy Park neighborhood was part of a farm belonging to Peter Stuyvesant (1612–1672), the last Dutch director general of New Netherlands. He purchased the land in 1651 from the Dutch West India Company. New Netherlands was ceded to the English in 1664 and renamed New York, and Stuyvesant retired to his farm in the woods (his *bouwerij*). The Bouweri Road, which originated as a Lenape Indian path, connected his farm to Fort New Amsterdam in Lower Manhattan. Over time, the name of the road changed from the Dutch Bouwerij Road (Farm Road) to the Bowery, and Stuyvesant's descendants sold his estate piecemeal.

In 1674, Peter Stuyvesant's widow, Judith, sold four acres of the land that now is part of Gramercy Park to Francisco Bastien, a freed African slave. The transaction was approved by the Dutch authorities because it was made during a short period when the Dutch regained possession of Manhattan island and renamed it New Orange. Bastien also purchased a fifteen-acre plot at Thirty-fourth Street and Sixth Avenue in 1684. In 1712, an English law was passed in New York denying blacks, Native Americans and mulattos the right to inherit or transfer land to their heirs. Bastien was the last black landowner in colonial lower Manhattan, and he had passed away before 1712. His heirs sold the land back to the Stuyvesant family (since they could no longer leave it to their descendants).

James De Lancey bought part of the Stuyvesant estate north of today's East Twentieth Street and sold it to his brother-in-law John Watts Sr. (1715–

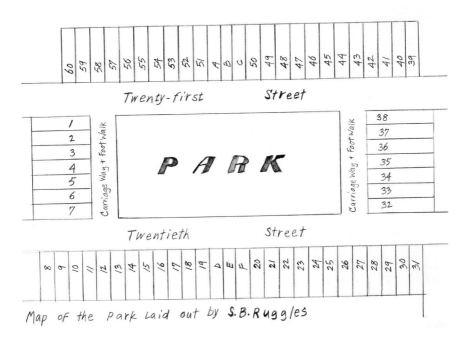

Map of the Park Laid out by S.B. Ruggles

Gramercy Park map laid out by Ruggles.

1789), who established his Rose Hill Farm on the land in 1747. De Lancey became lieutenant governor of New York in the 1750s, and the largest statue in the cemetery adjacent to Trinity Church (at Broadway and Wall Streets) is that of John Watts Jr. (1749–1836), a New York lawyer and politician who was elected to the U.S. Congress and later became a Westchester county judge—so you might say that right at its genesis, Gramercy Park was distinguished by well-known, influential New Yorkers. And it continues.

James Duane (1733–1797) purchased the four acres once owned by Francisco Bastien, plus ten adjoining acres of Rose Hill and built his Gramercy Farm in 1761. It was also called Gramercy Seat. The name Gramercy, it is believed, derived from the Dutch word *Crommessie*, part of an old Stuyvesant deed to the land that dated from 1697 that referred to a Crommessie Vly also known as Cedar Creek. The notion is that Gramercy is simply the Anglicized version of the Dutch word *Crommessie*.

While the English forces held New York during the American Revolution, Gramercy Seat was occupied by the British major general Daniel Jones and the commander of the British fleet, Admiral Robert Digby, from 1776 to 1783. After the Revolution, James Duane once again took possession of Gramercy Seat and enlarged his farm. Duane had been a delegate to the Continental Congress, a signer of the Articles of Confederation and the Continental Association before the Revolution and became New York City's first mayor after the Revolution and later a New York state senator.

It was Duane's five children who inherited, mortgaged and, by 1830, lost the Gramercy Park land to Jane Renwick (grandmother of architect James Renwick, who designed Grace Church and St. Patrick's Cathedral).

Now we are approaching the time when the Gramercy Farm land was developed into a wealthy urban neighborhood. This happened when a precocious young lawyer named Samuel Ruggles came to Manhattan and acquired the land he needed to develop Gramercy Square, Stuyvesant Square, Union Square and Madison Square as four separate residential neighborhoods. Ruggles was inspired by his earlier visits to St. John's Park in lower Manhattan, which had been modeled after an eighteenth-century London residential square, a park surrounded by mansions. The four residential developments became known as Manhattan's Four Squares.

Ruggles was born in Connecticut in 1800, and his family moved to Poughkeepsie, New York, when he was a small boy. He was accepted into Yale as a sophomore at the age of twelve and graduated at the age of fourteen, the youngest member of his class. A few years later, when he was licensed to practice law, Ruggles moved to Manhattan and opened an office on Prince Street. In May 1832, he married Mary Rosalie Rathbone, and it was their daughter, Ellen, who married George Templeton Strong in 1848. Samuel Ruggles gave the couple a lot at 55 Gramercy Park North, and George's father, George Washington Strong, built the couple's home on the lot.

George Templeton Strong (1820–1875), a lawyer and early prominent resident of Gramercy Park, graduated with high honors from Columbia College, of which he later became a trustee. Strong was a vestryman at the prestigious Trinity Church (Wall Street and Broadway), a founder of the Union League Club of New York and an early president of the New York Philharmonic Society and a gifted pianist, but he is most remembered as a diarist. From the time he was fifteen years of age and then for nearly forty years, Strong recorded a remarkable day-by-day personal account of events and life in the nineteenth century, especially during the era of the Civil War. His 2,250-page diary was discovered in the 1930s and is now held by the New York Historical Society. It is quoted by historians, and excerpts are featured in the documentary *The Civil War* by Ken Burns and in Ric Burn's *New York: A Documentary*.

During the chaotic decade leading up to and during the Civil War, George and Ellen Strong worked endlessly raising money for the Union.

Their fundraising for the Union took them to many Northern cities, including Poughkeepsie, New York, George's boyhood home, where they raised $16,000 (about $1.00 per citizen). Their ongoing efforts included fairs on Union Square, a cattle show on West Fifteenth Street and Seventh Avenue that raised $1 million and numerous other fundraising activities. George worked hard raising monies for the newly formed Sanitary Commission, which made drastic improvements with the sanitary conditions at Union army camps. The commission greatly increased the number of ambulances and medical supplies, attracted more badly needed surgeons to the military, employed hospital boats and improved medical care in every area. Ellen Strong served as a volunteer nurse on hospital ships. Some of the other Gramercy Park residents who participated in these efforts were Dr. Bellows, Reverend H. Bellows, Cyrus West Field, David Dudley Field and Peter Cooper.

In the entire history of New York City, there is nothing that was as brutal, tragic or shameful as the Draft Riots of July 1893. Politicians had encouraged violence, and mobs seized control of the city for four days as law and order broke down. Citizens, police and soldiers were tortured and killed.

The Conscription Act of 1863, with its provision that a well-to-do man could pay $300 for a substitute to take his place if he were drafted, along with the growing resentment and hatred for the newly freed blacks coming up from the South and competing with the Irish and other day laborers for work, mixed together with political rhetoric to incite the Draft Riots in Manhattan. The riots had their genesis with the Five Points gangs of Lower Manhattan. On July 13, 1863, an early manifestation of the riot started in front of the draft headquarters at East Forty-sixth Street and Third Avenue when the mob drove the police off and the building was burned down. The riot instantly spread throughout the city, causing well over one thousand deaths and the destruction of over $1.5 million worth of private property over a four-day period. Amid the robbing, looting and the burning of property, along with fierce bloody fighting—there were bodies hanging from lampposts and buildings—it was the abolitionists and blacks who were the mob's most frequent targets.

George Templeton Strong recorded in his diary that Police Superintendent Kennedy told him that over 1,155 persons had been killed. Strong also wrote that the residents of Gramercy Park were arming themselves, including the three Field households—David Dudley Field (Associate U.S. Supreme Court justice), his brother Cyrus West Field (an industrialist who laid the first Atlantic cable) and their father's household. All three were located on East Twenty-first Street (Gramercy Park North) and were prepared to defend themselves with muskets.

Lincoln had to dispatch about six thousand troops from Gettysburg (including West Point and Naval cadets) to put down the riot—and they did. The riot's final battle was fought in the Gramercy Park neighborhood on the night of July 16 when soldiers fought with marauders who were trying to break into and loot neighborhood homes. Thirteen men were killed before that confrontation ended. Considerable damage to the park itself was done, not by the rioters but because a large contingency of the militia had been encamped there.

In the following weeks, George Templeton Strong recorded in his diary the feelings of bitter exasperation he encountered in most New Yorkers. Their anger was not limited to the rioters but was equally directed toward the politicians whose rhetoric incited the riot, including New York State governor Horatio Seymour (he lost his governorship in the election of 1863 and later was the unsuccessful Democratic nominee in the 1868 presidential race). Social historian Herbert Asbury wrote, "Conservative estimates placed the total at two thousand killed and about eight thousand wounded." The riots instigated a response from the Republican Union League Club. Within eight months, the club members recruited, organized, trained and financed the Twentieth Regiment United States Colored Troops to fight in the Civil War.

On April 3, 1865, when the news that General Lee evacuated Richmond, Virginia, reached New York, everyone knew that the Confederacy was defeated. It was not yet official, but everyone was celebrating the fact that the war was won. The mood of the city was that of rejoicing, relief and gratitude that the war was over. One story illustrates the mood of the city. On April 6, 1865, a young Confederate officer escaped from Castle Williams military prison on Governor's Island and swam 3,200 feet to Manhattan, stepping over a seawall at the Battery, dripping wet in his gray Confederate uniform. A passerby asked him how he happened to fall into the bay. The young officer identified himself as Captain William R. Webb of the Second North Carolina Cavalry and stated, "I swam…I escaped from the prison stockade over there," and pointed. The civilian laughed and went on his way. For three days, the young officer wandered around the city. He looked a bit strange or out of place in his uniform and was occasionally questioned. He always identified himself as an escaped Confederate officer, but no one bothered to report him to the authorities. Who cared? The war was won.

In his home on Gramercy Park North, George T. Strong describes in his diary what it was like on April 3, when he first heard the news of Lee's evacuation of Richmond: "Never before did I hear cheering that came straight from the heart…I walked about on the outskirts of the crowd, shaking hands with everybody, congratulating and being congratulated by scores of men I hardly even knew by sight. Men embraced and hugged each other, kissed each other, retreated into doorways to dry their tears and came out again to flourish their hats and hurrah."

On April 9, 1865, it was official. General Lee surrendered to General Grant in Appomattox Court House in Virginia.

The Gramercy Park neighborhood was just recovering from the traumas of the Civil War when it was struck with the news that the brother of its most famous resident had assassinated Abraham Lincoln. Edwin Booth, America's greatest tragic stage actor, was living in the Gramercy Park neighborhood (at 107 East Seventeenth Street) on April 14, 1865, when his younger brother John Wilkes Booth assassinated Abraham Lincoln. Edwin (a Union sympathizer) wrote a public letter of apology and retired from the stage for about a year. Edwin's popularity was so strong that despite his brother's treason, he soon reestablished himself as America's most popular dramatic star. By 1869, Booth was able to build his own state-of-the-art theater on the southeast corner of West Twenty-third Street and Sixth Avenue, and by 1889, he had a mansion on Gramercy Park South that was redesigned by Stanford White. Later, Booth donated his mansion to the Players Club. In the late 1870s, Samuel Tilden, the governor of New York and the unsuccessful Democratic candidate in the 1876 presidential race, also built his mansion (designed by Calvert Vaux) on Gramercy Park South. It was finished in 1884, adjacent to Booth's mansion.

Both buildings became elite private clubs that led the Gramercy Park neighborhood into the twentieth century with their well-known membership that included three U.S. presidents: Theodore Roosevelt, Woodrow Wilson and Dwight D. Eisenhower. Membership also included such distinguished painters as Robert Henri, Frederic Remington, William Merritt Chase and Cecilia Beaux, along with such sculptors as Augustus Saint-Gaudens, Daniel Chester French, Anna Hyatt Huntington and Paul Manship. Members also included Victor Herbert, conductor Walter Damrosch, photographer Alfred Stieglitz and architects Stanford White and George B. Post. All were members of the National Arts Club at 15 Gramercy Park South, which also is known for its wide American art collection, with works by Edward Potthast, Francis Mora, Ella Lamb, Charles Curran, Henry Watrous, Oscar Fehrer, Helen Turner and Will Barnet and many others. The club also features innovative art media such as photography, film and digital media.

The Players Club, at 16 Gramercy Park South, was founded by Edwin Booth and fifteen others, including General William T. Sherman, John Drew and Mark Twain, with its purpose to promote social intercourse between members of the dramatic profession and the kindred professions of literature, painting, architecture, sculpture and music, law and medicine and the patrons of the arts.

Former members include: George M. Cohan, William Astor Chanler, Stanford White, Nikola Tesla, John Barrymore, Eugene O'Neill, James Cagney, Gregory Peck, Alfred Lunt, Robert M. McBride, Walter Cronkite, Alexander Woollcott, Kevin Spacey, Judy Collins, Rue McClanahan, George S. Kaufman, Angela Lansbury, Sidney Poitier, Tony Bennett, Tony Roberts, Carol Burnett, Liza Minnelli, Dick Cavett, Billy Connolly, Vartan Gregorian, Hal Holbrook, George Innes, Eli Wallach, Robert Vaughn, Ben Gazzara, Christopher Plummer, Budd Schulberg, Ethan Hawke, Jimmy Fallon, Marian Seldes, Peter O'Toole, Rosemary Harris, Roger Moore, Russell Miller and Sidney Zion. These club members blended nicely and contributed a certain prestige to the surrounding Gramercy Park neighborhood, even though they departed from the strictly residential nature of Gramercy Park up to that point in time.

There were other private clubs on Gramercy Park, including the Netherlander Club at 3 Gramercy Park West from 1912 to 1939; the Columbia University Club from 1905 to 1918 and the Army & Navy Club from 1918 to about 1927, both at 18 Gramercy Park South; and a few others. But of all the clubs, the Players and the National Art clubs exercised the most influence in the neighborhood not only because they predated the other clubs on the park but also because they are the ones that survive to this day. Over time, they were the most popular of all the clubs on the park.

At the turn of the last century, while these two clubs were taking hold in Gramercy Park, there was another development that gradually established a presence and slowly altered Gramercy Park's character for over 130 years and continues to this day. That was the Gramercy, Gramercy Park's first apartment house, which opened at 34 Gramercy Park East in 1883. Gramercy Park's next apartment building opened in 1909 at 24 Gramercy Park South. It was followed by 36 Gramercy Park East and 50 Gramercy Park North in 1910, and then came the Gramercy Park Hotel in 1920 and 44 Gramercy Park North apartments in 1930. A few more apartment buildings sprang up around the park in the following decades. Now jumping ahead to the twenty-first century, we have had a flurry of luxury apartment house development. The Gramercy Park Hotel was converted to condominiums and a boutique hotel along with 50 Gramercy Park North in 2007 and 18 Gramercy Park South in 2011.

One block south of Gramercy Park South, we have East Nineteenth Street between Irving Place and Third Avenue, where rows of brick and brownstone homes went up between 1840 and the 1850s. Located in the neighborhood of Gramercy Park (and part of today's Gramercy Park Historic District), these homes were thought of as upper-class homes in the neighborhood. But by 1900, they were aging houses, and the block was slipping quickly into a lower middle-class or working-class area. Then along came Frederick Sterner, an architect born in the 1860s in London, who immigrated to the United States in 1882 and practiced architecture in Colorado before moving to New York in 1906. Sterner rented an office on Fifth Avenue near Nineteenth Street and a house at 23 West Twentieth Street while he searched for his own house. At the time, well-to-do Victorian gentry were moving north and shunned neighborhoods that were already developed. Sterner was attracted by the lower prices on East Nineteenth Street. He purchased a house at 139 East Nineteenth Street and remodeled it with a coat of tinted stucco, shutters, decorative ironwork and a projecting tile roof—elements that became part of his signature remodeling style.

Sterner's home attracted Joseph P. Thomas (a banker and polo player), who hired Sterner to remodel a plain Greek Revival house at 135 East Nineteenth Street into a picturesque Gothic house (some called it picturesque Mediterranean in style). The block was getting a slightly bohemian flavor, as Sterner purchased a few more houses on the block and other owners on the block hired Sterner to redesign their homes. At least eight houses were remodeled, and an apartment building at 132 East Nineteenth Street was remodeled by Sterner in a half-timbered style. Sterner's brother Albert, a painter, moved into 132 East Nineteenth Street. The block was attracting successful artists, actors and writers, including Ida Tarbell, Theda Bara, Robert Winthrop Chanler, Mrs. Patrick Campbell, Oleg Cassini, Lincoln Kirstein, George Wolfe, Cecilia Beaux, Edward Brit (Ted) Husing, George Bellows, Carl Van Vechten and many others.

In 1914, Harriet Gillespie described the East Nineteenth Street block as "Block Beautiful" in an article for *American Homes and Gardens* magazine, and the name stuck. In 1921, Helen Lowery in an article for the *New York Times* credited Sterner with the idea of how to revive older neighborhoods for upper-class people. She described Sterner's style of remodeling as a picturesque Italian front on a house. Turtle Bay Gardens and Sutton Place are examples of Sterner's influence.

There is much more that can be told about Gramercy Park's historic district and its surrounding neighborhood, but its time to start the walking tour.

Chapter 2

OUR TOUR BEGINS

East Seventeenth Street and Third Avenue

We are starting the tour at the northeast corner of East Seventeenth Street and Third Avenue. If we look across Third Avenue at 190 Third Avenue, we will see Scheffel Hall. It was also known as Joe King's Rathskeller and is a New York City landmark. It opened in 1895 as a German beer hall designed by Henry Adam Weber and Hubert Drosser in a German Renaissance Revival style with an elaborately detailed terra-cotta façade that is strongly influenced by the well-known Friedrichsbau Castle at Heidelberg, Germany (now an educational institution). It features intricate strap, jewel work designs, diamond rustication and cartouches. Also, on top, we see a curved front roof gable and richly decorated window surrounds. All come together for a distinctive ornate design. Its founder was Carl Goerwitz, an immigrant from Germany in 1873.

It is the type of building people stop and stare at, wondering what it was originally. The beer garden Scheffel Hall was named for the German poet, novelist and lawyer Joseph Victor von Scheffel, best remembered for *Gaudeamus*, a collection of short songs.

William Sydney Porter (O. Henry) lived around the corner on Irving Place and frequented the beer hall, as he did any number of neighborhood bars. He used Scheffel Hall as a setting for his 1909 short story set in a German restaurant: "The Halberdier of the Little Rheinschloss."

The beer hall was located just north of a part of the Lower East Side that was known as *Kleindeutchland*, or Little Germany, until 1902, when the *General Slocum* disaster caused a mass movement of the German American families

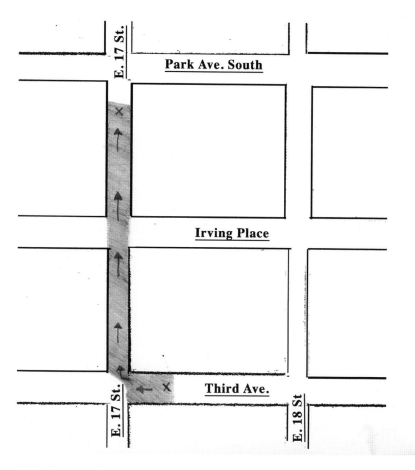

Map of East Seventeenth Street.

to new neighborhoods (mostly to Yorkville). The surviving family members were trying to forget the tragic losses of their children, mothers, daughters and wives who perished in the disaster, about 1,100 women and children all from Little Germany and all going on a weekday Arbor Day outing. The *General Slocum* steamboat burned and sank at Hell's Gate under the span where today's Triborough Bridge is located.

The beer hall has changed hands many times over the past one hundred years. It has been a bar and a restaurant, and in 1928, an athletic club took over the building. Later, it reopened again as a bar and a restaurant. In the 1970s, Fat Tuesdays, a popular jazz club, opened here and lasted until the early part of the twenty-first century. It is currently a yoga and pilates studio.

If we walk west on East Seventeenth Street toward Irving Place, on the north side of the street at 143 East Seventeenth Street, we see St. John the Baptist Church, a Greek Orthodox church that opened in 1885. The architect was Schwartman & Buchman, and the church has a Baroque façade that was altered in 1957 and again in 2004. The interior was redesigned in 2010.

Farther down the same block in 1922, the ground floor at 141 East Seventeenth Street was a grocery store (now a bicycle shop), and there were apartments above. Sharing an apartment here were two recent Yale graduates, Henry Luce (1898–1967) and Briton Hadden (1898–1929). It was here where they conceived the idea for *Time* magazine, and having raised $86,000 of their $100,000 goal, they published the first issue in March 1922. Henry Luce was business manager, and Hadden was editor in chief, and they annually rotated the titles of president and secretary-treasurer. After Hadden died suddenly at the age of thirty-one in 1929, Luce assumed all of the above-mentioned positions.

Hadden became ill and died of heart failure because it seems that streptococcus viridans entered his bloodstream, causing septicemia. Hadden made a will that left all of his stock in Time Inc. to his mother and forbade his family from selling the stock shares for forty-nine years. Within a year, Luce formed a syndicate and succeeded in gaining hold of Hadden's stock.

As we continue down East Seventeenth Street to 129 East Seventeenth Street, we see Manhattan's oldest surviving apartment building, which opened in 1879. The building is five stories and has a brick and brownstone, mild-mannered Gothic Revival façade designed by Napoleon Le Brun (1821–1901).

Apartment houses are referred to as a separate class of residential building from tenements. Apartment houses had middle-class amenities such as windows, hallways and bathroom facilities in each apartment that were absent in the tenements built primarily for poor immigrants and their families.

When we reach the southeast corner of East Seventeenth Street and Irving Place, there is a colossal bronze bust of Washington Irving that was dedicated in 1885 in Bryant Park. It was rededicated on October 29, 1939, in front of Washington Irving High School, at 40 Irving Place. The sculptor was Friedrich Beer (1846–1912), and the bust was a gift from a German admirer, Dr. Joseph Wiener. The bust is part of the collection of the City of New York and was initially intended for Central Park, but it went to Bryant Park instead, where it stayed until the 1930s, when Bryant Park was redesigned with WPA funds, and the bust was moved here.

It is a realistic portrait of an old Washington Irving, with sagging facial muscles and a thoughtful expression. Although the features and general characteristics of Washington Irving's bust may be slightly faulty, his likeness in general is well preserved. This work was considered successful in model and workmanship by most, but some, like Daniel Huntington of the National Academy of Design, feel that the work fails to convey Irving's "dignity" or refinement of expression.

Washington Irving (1783–1859) used the pseudonym Diedrich Knickerbocker and was the first American Man of Letters, a writer to achieve international fame and recognition and to earn his living solely as a writer. From 1802 to 1859, Irving had over eighteen of his works published successfully, and his best remembered stories include "Rip Van Winkle," "The Legend of Sleepy Hollow" in 1820 and *Knickerbocker's History of New York* in 1809. Irving's best-known characters were Rip Van Winkle and Ichabod Crane.

Behind the bust of Washington Irving, we see Washington Irving High School, opened in 1913 and named for Washington Irving. It was designed by superintendent Charles B.J. Snyder with a simple Renaissance façade. The high school was a progressive educator's dream, the first technical school for girls with everything in one building. The school became co-ed in 1986.

The interior spaces are Collegiate Gothic and spectacular, with a massive two-story wood-carved foyer decorated with a series of several murals and sculptures, including twelve murals by Barry Faulkner depicting twelve scenes from Washington Irving's *Knickerbocker's History of New York*, dated 1917 to 1921. Here is a partial list that gives you an idea of the subject matter included in the murals:

- A panel by Robert Knight of the colonial Dutch trading with Indians, located in the Gothic-styled auditorium
- Twelve narrow female figures by J. Mortimer Lichtenauer (1932) representing ideas (heads up) and work (heads down)
- Salvatore Lascari's 1932 murals over the stairs depicting scenes of old and new Manhattan from the first to third floors, as well as others in the cafeteria

The high school gave us such well-known actresses as Claudette Colbert (Emily Claudette Chauchoin), who graduated in the class of 1921 with an interest in fashion, design and art. While attending the school, she appeared in several school plays, and in 1923, Claudette Chauchoin appeared in a play at the Provincetown Playhouse in Greenwich Village. By 1935, she was

Claudette Colbert and won an Oscar for best actress in *It Happened One Night*. Sylvia Miles (Sylvia Lee) attended Washington Irving High School in the 1940s and was nominated for an Academy Award in 1968 for best supporting actress in *Midnight Cowboy* and again in 1975 for *Farewell My Lovely*. Whoopi Goldberg (Caryn Johnson) attended the school in the 1960s and dropped out. She won an Academy Award for best actress in *The Color Purple*.

The Washington Irving school campus is now shared by four independent schools: Washington Irving High School, the High School for Language and Diplomacy, Gramercy Arts High School and the Academy for Software Engineering.

Unfortunately, despite its rich history, Washington Irving High School is scheduled to be closed by summer 2015 because of a graduation rate of 48 percent, and the Success Academy Charter Schools Group plans to open an elementary school in the building.

Before Washington Irving High School was built, this was the site of the National Conservatory of Music of America. Antonin Dvorak was its director from 1893 to 1895, and Victor Herbert was a teacher here.

Across Irving Place at the southwest corner of East Seventeenth Street starts the East Seventeenth Street/Irving Place Historic District, which consists of ten residential buildings that run along the south side of East Seventeenth Street from 122 East Seventeenth Street (aka 49 Irving Place) to 104 East Seventeenth Street.

The building at 122 East Seventeenth Street is architecturally distinctive in the historic district because of its canopied porch, intricate entranceway and cast ironwork added when the 1847 Greek Revival house was remodeled between 1853 and 1854. Between 1864 and 1886, it was home to Charles A. and Sarah Macy. He was a banker and an uncle of the founder of Macy's Department Stores. Other well-known residents of the house were Elsie de Wolfe (an actress, interior decorator and author) and theatrical agent Elizabeth Marbury, who lived here from 1892 to 1911. They were said to be the most fashionable lesbian couple of the Victorian era, and they held a popular weekly salon (meetings) here attended by well-known entertainers, politicians, socialites, newspaper people and other carefully selected guests. These salons featured lively discussions of the topics of the day. Elsie and Elizabeth were known as the "bachelors" and had as their motto "never complain, never explain," which Elsie embroidered on silk pillows that were copied and sold by shops across the country.

Ella "Elsie" Anderson de Wolfe was born in New York City in 1865 and died in France 1950. She spent her childhood in the British Isles and was

MISS ELSIE DE WOLFE.

Photo by Miss Ben Yusuf.

MISS DE WOLFE, WHO AS AN AMIABLE GHOST IN HER NEW PLAY, "THE SHADES OF NIGHT," HAS "CAUGHT THE TOWN."

Elsie De Wolfe in 1901. *Courtesy of the Library of Congress.*

presented at the English royal court. In 1884, she returned to New York City, where she became a professional actress by 1890. In 1905, Elsie de Wolfe turned to interior decoration, and she is credited with becoming the first professional interior decorator. At that time, interior decorating was done by an architect or someone who sold furniture or antiques. Elsie de Wolfe's reputation was initially established by her imaginative interior design for the Colony Club, which opened in 1907 on Madison Avenue in Manhattan. It was the first important woman's club in New York. Elsie obtained the commission through her friendship with Stanford White, who had been hired to design the Colony Club. He recommended her and dismissed the club's initial objection because of her apparent lack of experience. "Give it to Elsie," he said firmly, "and let the girl alone! She knows more than any of us." And thus Elsie de Wolfe got her first important commission. Her list of well-known clients came to include Anne Morgan, the Duke and Duchess of Windsor, philanthropist Elizabeth Milbank Anderson, Adelaide and Henry Clay Frick and Anne Vanderbilt, among others. Elsie's use of eighteenth-century French furniture and reproductions along with brighter colors and light made her designs dramatically change the Victorian interiors of wealthy homes.

Besides being an actress and an interior decorator Elsie marched in a Fifth Avenue parade for women's suffrage in 1912, and her books *The House in Good Taste*, published in 1913, and *After All* helped her become nationally known. Elsie married English royalty Lord Charles Mendl, becoming Lady Mendl. After World War II, she returned to France.

Elizabeth Marbury (1856–1933) was born in a home on the site of 76 Irving Place (now an apartment building constructed in 1910 with small statues of babies over its entrance). Elizabeth grew up in the Gramercy Park area and made an important career for herself representing famous European writers in the United States, and she often served as producer for their works on stage. Two of the more well-known foreign writers Elizabeth represented were George Bernard Shaw and Oscar Wilde. Wilde stayed at 47 Irving Place and visited Elizabeth and Elsie in 1893 while he was on a lecture tour in New York and his play *Vera* was being rehearsed at a theater on Union Square. Elizabeth Marbury's clients covered a wide range of talented writers and artists to the dance team of Vernon & Irene Castle, and she also was an early promoter of African American writers of the Harlem Renaissance. Marbury's influence on the development of the Broadway musical is often overlooked. Her modern "Book Musicals" that she produced in the nineteenth century came to be known as "Broadway

Musicals" by audiences in the twentieth century. And through her American Play company, Marbury produced Cole Porter's first musical, *See America First*, which opened in Providence, Rhode Island; New Haven, Connecticut; and Schenectady, Albany and Rochester, New York, before coming to Broadway in 1916.

Before Cole Porter's Broadway musical, Marbury produced Jerome Kern's *Nobody Home* in 1915, along with *Very Good, Eddie* in 1915 and *Love o' Mike* in 1916.

Elizabeth Marbury never married but lived openly for more than twenty years with Elsie de Wolfe. Marbury died in 1933. Her funeral at St. Patrick's Cathedral was attended by an array of the most important American leaders and dignitaries of the day. Elsie de Wolfe was not at the funeral, but she was the prime beneficiary of Marbury's will.

The Irving opened at 118 East Seventeenth Street in 1902, replacing a row house, and was the last building constructed in the historic district. This six-story, twenty-foot-wide, flats building, designed by Alfred E. Badt with Renaissance Revival details, attracted working-class or middle-class tenants who were less prominent than the tenants at the Fanwood. Both apartment buildings were similar in scale and complementary in detail to the older row houses on the block.

As we walk toward Union Square on East Seventeenth Street, we are passing 116 East Seventeenth Street. In the late 1880s, as the block's residential population was changing, this row house was the block's first conversion of a single-family house to a boardinghouse.

The Fanwood Apartments opened at 112–114 East Seventeenth Street in 1891, replacing two row houses. Architect George F. Pelham designed the six-story apartment building in a Romanesque/Renaissance Revival style, with projecting rock-faced brownstone bands on a two-story brownstone base with a large entrance portico. The façade is brick with brownstone trim from the third to the sixth floors and has a three-story arcade rising from the third to the fifth floors. The 1898 alteration added an iron-galvanized cornice that has more Renaissance characteristics than the rest of the building.

Because of the changes in the neighborhood after World War I, several of the houses on the block were converted to accommodate studio apartments and other multiple-dwelling uses. Stoops were removed, and ground-level entrances were created at 106 and 108 East Seventeenth Street. The last exclusively single-family occupancy house on the block was 120 East Seventeenth Street, which converted to multiple dwellings in 1936.

The building at 108 East Seventeenth Street was home to William R. Grace (1832–1904) and his wife, Lillius, from 1873 to 1880. Grace was a wealthy capitalist and a founder of W.R. Grace & Co. and Grace Institute. Grace was an immigrant, shipping magnate and the first Irish-born mayor and the first Catholic mayor (elected in 1880 and again in 1884) of New York.

In 1897, he founded Grace Institute as a tuition-free training program to educate and find employment for women in need. Throughout the twentieth century and to this day, Grace Institute provides low-income and unemployed women with the skills training and job placement help they need to become economically self-sufficient.

This historic district is a cohesive enclave in that its buildings have a similarity in their scale, materials and decorative details and there is a social and cultural history that, at various points in time, connected the block with its surrounding Gramercy Park neighborhood and with Union Square.

Not part of the historic district on the opposite side of the street, at the site of 107 East Seventeenth Street is where the home of Edwin Booth (1833–1893), America's greatest tragic stage actor, was located. In 1863, after his truly beloved first wife, Mary, died, he was grief stricken and moved here with his mother, Maryann (Holmes), his sister Rosalie and his young daughter, Edwina. For Edwin, nothing would ever change the moment on the train when he realized Mary was gone. Edwin went to spiritualists trying to contact his dead wife, with whom he had had two and a half years of happiness—such a short time. Edwin decided to stop

Edwin Booth. *Courtesy of the Library of Congress.*

drinking and devote himself to making a life for Edwina. He eventually had to travel as he returned to the stage so he could give his daughter all she needed, and Edwina stayed here under the care of Rosalie and Maryann. In Edwin's own words, Edwina became "the light of [his] darkened life." On his return to the theater, he took his sorrow to the stage and filled his roles with breathtaking levels of tragic authority. It was about two years later, on April 14, 1865, that his brother John Wilkes Booth assassinated Abraham Lincoln. The Civil War had split the Booth family in half. Edwin Booth and his sister Asia were strong supporters of the Union, while their brothers John Wilkes Booth and Junius Brutus Booth Jr. were strong supporters of the Confederacy.

Ironically, while touring in 1864, Edwin was at the Jersey City railroad station when he saw a young man buy a ticket for a sleeping berth from the conductor on the platform. A crowd rushed in, and the train started moving as the young man was knocked about and twisted off his feet. He fell between the platform and the car, helpless and in immediate danger of being crushed. Edwin jumped forward and grabbed his coat collar and arm, pulling him to safety. The young man recognized him and said, "That was a close call, Mr. Booth." Edwin, who was shy off the stage, always hated to be recognized in public and quickly went on his way. A few weeks later, he learned the young man he had rescued was Robert Todd Lincoln—the president's son.

The structure at 121 East Seventeenth Street is a former Early Romanesque Revival–style carriage house that was built about 1854 for J.O. Ward (resident of 51 Irving Place). The structure has had many uses, including as a garage, restaurant, office and residence, but it still possesses many of its original details.

Chapter 3

ARTISTS, WRITERS AND MORE

IRVING PLACE TO EAST NINETEENTH STREET

If we walk back to Irving Place and head to the corner of East Sixteenth Street, we will pass 47 Irving Place, where Oscar Wilde (1854–1900) stayed (as mentioned in the previous chapter) in 1883. On the northwest corner of East Sixteenth Street and Irving Place, there once was the Westminster Hotel, where in 1876 the Westminster Kennel Club was organized. Charles Dickens (1812–1870) stayed at the hotel during his reading tour in 1867. Across the street at 33 Irving Place, the oldest magazine in the United States, the *Nation*, moved its offices upstairs in this building in 1998. The magazine has been active since 1865 and has had such well-known contributors as Henry James, Leon Trotsky, H.L. Mencken, Albert Einstein, George Orwell, I.F. Stone, Jean-Paul Sartre, Martin Luther King, James Baldwin and Hunter S. Thompson.

And now we continue between East Seventeenth Street and East Eighteenth Street and stop in front of 54 and 56 Irving Place. We will notice two nice Greek Revival, brick, single-family row houses built between 1841 and 1843 that remain intact with their original high stoops, their massive temple-like brownstone entrance enframements and simple stone window lintels and sills. No. 56 Irving Place has wrought-iron and cast-iron stoop railings and a cornice with dentals. No. 54 Irving Place was altered in 1879, with a Neo-Grec oriel window and cornice. By the early twentieth century, 54 Irving Place was home to the Ingersoll Club and 56 Irving Place had been converted to a boardinghouse. In 1921, 54 Irving Place was converted to the Cooperative Cafeteria and expanded into 56 Irving Place in 1924. This

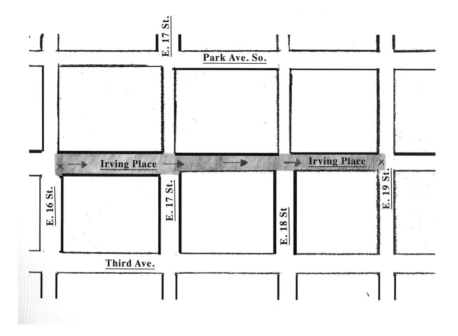

Map of Irving Place.

was a project of Consumers' Cooperative Services (CCC), one of several organizations founded shortly after World War I, created to provide working people with quality services like restaurants, shops, housing and more at reasonable prices. The cafeteria had a kitchen in the basement and dining rooms in the basement and on the first floor. The upper floors had offices, staff living quarters and guest rooms. Eventually, the cafeteria was replaced by a number of different commercial enterprises.

The two buildings now house the Inn, also known as the Inn on Irving, and include Cibar (a pink lounge), along with a Victorian tea house named Lady Mendl's Tea Room & Dessert Parlor, named after Elsie de Wolfe, who lived at 49 Irving Place and became Lady Mendl. The Inn is an unmarked, secretive, deluxe twelve-suite hotel, furnished with exquisite antiques reminiscent of Edith Wharton's New York and includes the modern comforts of remote climate control, computers with Internet access and more. Each suite has a sitting room that simulates the elegance of the Gilded Age. Breakfast can be enjoyed in bed or in the Inn's guest parlor.

Between Seventeenth and Eighteenth Streets, at 55 Irving Place, there is a plaque on the entrance commemorating the fact that from 1903 to 1907,

O. Henry lived in a building that used to be on this site in a street-level apartment, with a fireplace and a bay window in which he sat one day and wrote "The Gift of the Magi" in four hours. Supposedly, he got the idea for the story while drinking at Healy's (now Pete's Tavern). O. Henry had moved into the Gramercy Park neighborhood around the time he was hired by *New York World* to write weekly stories at $100 for each story. Gramercy Park appeared in many of his stories, such as "The Discounters of Money,"

O. Henry. *Original pen and ink drawing by Ann Woodward.*

about an aristocratic family that receives a key to the park, and "The Trimmed Lamp," a story about two young working girls, Nancy and Lou. In the tale, the former friends meet at the park's gate. Nancy now believes in honesty and generosity, while Lu, dressed in furs and jewels, is a rich man's mistress. When Nancy tells Lu that she is engaged to the man Lu discarded, Lu realizes the terrible mistake she made and crumbles at the foot of the gate, sobbing uncontrollably.

O. Henry is a pseudonym created by William Sydney Porter (1862–1910). In February 1898, William Sidney Porter was found guilty of embezzlement and was sentenced on March 25, 1898, to be imprisoned at the Ohio Penitentiary in Columbus. He worked in the prison hospital as the night druggist and had his own room in the hospital wing. While in prison, he had fourteen stories published under various pseudonyms. The pseudonym O. Henry first appeared with the story "Whistling Dick's Christmas Stocking" in a December 1899 issue of *McClure's Magazine*, and it soon became the most popular of his pen names. Porter's pseudonym O. Henry was an acronym he created from the name of the prison (**Oh**io Penit**en**tia**ry**) where he was incarcerated. O. Henry's friend in New Orleans sent his stories to publishers so they would have no idea the writer was in prison. Porter was released on July 24, 1901, for good behavior after serving three years of a five-year sentence.

To understand how popular his stories were, you have to know that by the time he died in 1910 at forty-eight years old, over 50 million copies of his books had been sold in the United States. Many of his stories were inspired by life in New York City and are remembered for their wit, wordplay, warm characterizations and clever twist endings.

Near the southeast corner of Irving Place, at the site of 136 East Eighteenth Street, stood the home of the English-born architect Calvert Vaux (1824–1895) who, from 1857 to 1858, along with Frederick Law Olmsted, created Greensward, the plan that was chosen for the creation of Central Park. Vaux (standing four feet, eleven inches tall) came to New York as a landscape architect working for Andrew Jackson Downing and soon became a partner in Downing's firm in the early 1850s. Vaux was an equal partner with Frederick Law Olmsted in designing Central Park, and although they never specified who designed any particular elements of Central Park, most historians credit Calvert Vaux with designing the original Victorian Gothic structures and bridges that were in the park when it opened.

As an architect working in Manhattan, Calvert Vaux designed the Samuel Tilden mansion at 16 Gramercy Park South, the Jefferson Market Courthouse (now the Jefferson Market Library) in 1873 at Sixth Avenue and West Ninth Street, the original buildings (no longer visible from the street) for the American Museum of Natural History and the Metropolitan Museum of Art. Also the architect of several buildings for the Children's Aid Society, most of his designs were in his distinctive, picturesque, Victorian Gothic style.

On the site of 142 East Eighteenth Street was built the first true apartment building in New York, the Stuyvesant Apartments, constructed in 1869 and demolished in 1957. The apartment building was designed by Richard Morris Hunt as a five-story walk-up for middle-class tenants. It became known as the first French flat and as a cornerstone for apartment house development in America.

At the time, middle-class New Yorkers preferred to rent or own row houses and were reluctant to accept apartment buildings (though they were popular in France), partly because they associated them with tenements built for poor immigrants. Tenements had communal toilets and small windowless rooms and no halls or kitchen facilities (only a potbellied stove supplied by the tenant) inside the apartment. The Stuyvesant corrected all of the above-mentioned shortcomings by including more and larger rooms with windows along with bathrooms, kitchen facilities and hallways inside each apartment.

Although the *Real Estate Record and Guide* in November 1869 predicted that "the average American is not prepared to live openly in part of a house" and would prefer a long commute to the suburbs, every apartment was rented

Nos. 135 to 143 East Eighteenth Street. Pre–Civil War Italianate homes from 1855.

before the building opened, and hundreds of applicants were turned away. The apartment building was built by Rutherford Stuyvesant (1843–1909), a descendant of Peter Stuyvesant.

The well-known French-American artist and sculptor Louise Bourgeois (1911–2010) lived at the Stuyvesant from the early 1940s to the early 1950s with her husband and three children. Louise worked in her apartment and on the roof of the Stuyvesant. She became one of the most important artists in modern and contemporary art and is probably best remembered for her spider structures, which gave her the nickname the "Spiderwoman."

Across the street on the south edge of the Gramercy Park Historic District, notice a row of pre–Civil War homes at 135 to 143 East Eighteenth Street. They were built in 1855 and are noteworthy because of the Italianate hooded lintels over their windows and because all but no. 141 have their original cast-iron newels, balustrades and fences.

In 1923, poet William Rose Benet (1885–1950) moved in at 143 East Eighteenth Street with his new wife, poet Elinor Wylie (1885–1928). They seemed to be a thought-provoking couple. Benet was born in Brooklyn, educated at Yale and was founder, editor and writer for the *Saturday Review of Literature*. Benet won the Pulitzer Prize for literature in 1942. His works include *Merchants from Cathay* (1913), *The Dust Which*

Is God (1941) and *With Wings as Eagles* (1940). His brother was poet and novelist Stephen Vincent Benet.

Elinor Wylie was a popular American poet and novelist almost as well known for her elegant, fragile beauty as she was for her sensuous, lyrical poetry. She was a bookish young girl who grew into a tall, dark beauty and became notorious in her social circles for her many affairs and marriages. She suffered through several miscarriages, a stillbirth and a premature child who died after one week. By 1928, Elinor's marriage to Benet was in trouble, and they agreed to live apart. Elinor moved to England and fell in love with the husband of a good friend, Henry de Clifford Woodhouse, to whom she wrote a series of nineteen sonnets. Elinor then returned to New York and moved back in with Benet, who was helping her prepare for publication the book *Angels and Earthly Creatures*, which included the sonnets to Woodhouse, when she died of a stroke at the age of forty-three.

At the southeast corner of Irving Place and East Eighteenth Street, we can see the first of many brown street signs (instead of the blue-green color of regular street signs) that indicate you are in a New York City historic district. The name of the historic district, Gramercy Park Historic District, appears in the narrow black area at the top of the sign.

Also at the southeast corner of East Eighteenth Street is 66 Irving Place, which opened as the Porter Hotel in 1829, with a grocery store on the ground floor. Around 1851, the grocery store was converted into a saloon. By 1864, it was fully listed as a saloon, and in 1899, Tom and John Healy purchased the tavern and renamed it Healy's, with a decorative six-point star over the entrance. In 1932, a man named Pete Belle purchased the tavern and renamed it Pete's Tavern, the name it retains to this day. It is considered New York City's second-oldest surviving bar. The Bridge Café, at 279 Water Street (on the corner of Dover Street), which opened in 1804, is the oldest surviving New York City bar. Healy's continued illegal operation as a speakeasy during Prohibition, using the Royal Flower Shop as a front.

Pete's Tavern (known as Healy's at the turn of the last century) appears in movies, television ads and in some of O. Henry's short stories, including "The Lost Blend." While O. Henry lived at 55 Irving Place, he frequented Healy's Tavern, though he was somewhat secretive, wearing a slouch hat, usually coming in around midnight and drinking quietly. The regulars at Healy's gave the bar the nickname "the Club," and O. Henry was definitely a member as he quietly studied the patrons and used them in one way or another in many of his stories. O. Henry wrote dozens of short stories every year—mostly intimate stories that depicted street people, shop girls, bums

Pete's Tavern, at the northeast corner of Irving Place and East Eighteenth Street.

and other ordinary people—and he used surprise endings to reinforce the sentimental glitter and pathos of their lives in the city.

Legend has it that in 1939, Ludwig Bemelmans (1898–1962), an Austria-Hungary-born American illustrator and writer of children books, was sitting in Pete's Tavern while writing the first of seven of what became the *Madeline* children's book series, his most famous. Bemelmans also wrote adult books, travel books, humorous works and movie scripts. His legacy includes murals on Aristotle Onassis's yacht *Christina*, along with a number of other paintings and murals in private collections. His only mural that is publicly displayed is *Central Park* on the walls of the Bemelmans Bar at the Carlyle Hotel in Manhattan.

Bemelmans's connection to the Gramercy neighborhood is secure because he was a good friend of Elsie de Wolfe, frequented the Players Club (16 Gramercy Park South) and the National Arts Club (15 Gramercy Park South), rented an apartment at the old Stuyvesant Fish mansion (19 Gramercy Park South) and lived at the Hotel Irving (26 Gramercy Park South). Bemelmans's last address in Gramercy Park was at the National Arts Club Studio Building (119 East Nineteenth Street), where he passed away. His book *Sunshine*, published in 1950, was a love letter to Gramercy Park and to New York.

No. 76 Irving Place is an apartment house that was built in 1910 and is distinctive at ground level because of small statues of babies over its entrance. In 1856, Elizabeth Marbury (see chapter 2) was born in a house previously on the site.

Across Irving Place is 71 Irving Place, built in 1846 and in 1945 was home to Norman Thomas (1884–1968) and his family. His wife Violet operated a tearoom on the ground floor from the mid-1930s into the 1940s. In 1944, Norman Thomas ran for president of the United States six times on the Socialist Party of America ticket. Thomas was a Presbyterian minister, a Socialist, a pacifist, a political writer and an activist. He was a founder of the National Civil Liberties Bureau, which was the precursor of the American Civil Liberties Union (ACLU). Norman Thomas was born and raised in Marion, Ohio, and graduated Princeton University with honors in 1905. He attended Union Theological Seminary, graduated and was ordained a Presbyterian minister in 1911.

Initially, Thomas was outspoken in opposing World War II, but after the United States was attacked at Pearl Harbor, he supported our involvement in the war and later wrote critically of his prior positions of not backing our earlier involvement in the war against the Nazis and overestimating the ability of non-fascist Europe to resist the Nazis. Thomas was one of the few public figures to openly oppose President Franklin Roosevelt's internment of Japanese Americans, and he accused the ACLU of "dereliction of duty" when the organization supported the internment. Norman Thomas campaigned against racial segregation, environmental depletion and anti-labor laws and practices and in favor of opening the United States to Jewish victims of Nazi persecution in the 1930s. Early on, Thomas came out in favor of birth control. He ran for several different political offices but never was elected to any. Norman Thomas's connection to the Gramercy Park neighborhood is strong because he lived at various addresses in the neighborhood, including 19 Gramercy Park South and at a house formerly at the site of 39½ Gramercy Park North.

Chapter 4

MUCKRAKERS AND ARCHITECTURE

East Nineteenth Street to
Park Avenue South

We will now walk one block north and take a careful look at 81 Irving Place, a fourteen-story apartment house that opened in 1930 at the northwest corner of East Nineteenth Street. George Pelham (1867–1937) is the architect who designed this robust building that proudly displays three distinctive styles of architecture.

The Setback style refers to the building's higher section with its many separate tiers, each set back from the one below, resulting in a shape like a wedding cake, sometimes referred to as wedding cake setbacks. At 81 Irving Place, the water tower is enclosed in a striking rooftop pavilion that becomes an intricate part of the setback design's distinguishing features.

The Arts and Craft style is distributed throughout the building's façade with the numerous intricate designs and patterns created by the building's brickwork and is accented by the façade's thick, glazed finish, which was accomplished by using a spray gun with two nozzles.

The Neo-Gothic style is represented by over a dozen large grotesque gargoyles that are overhanging its façade, along with the many fanciful and/ or grotesque motifs decorating this great building, including twisted columns, small atlantes, animal heads, monsters and other fantastic creatures.

The Setback style is unlike other styles in that it can be found on a wide range of historical and anti-historical-styled buildings constructed from the early twentieth century to the mid-twentieth century—including buildings that are historical or eclectic in style or buildings that are Art Moderne, Art Deco, Modern or the International style. The Setback style is almost

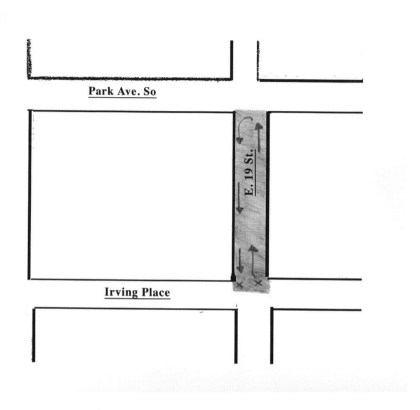

Map of East Nineteenth Street.

exclusive to New York City because of a 1916 zoning law that forced buildings there to reduce their shadow on the street.

At 120 East Nineteenth Street is a four-story Italianate fronted brownstone row house that was built about 1853 and is pretty much intact except for the removal of the stoop in 1923. It is similar to many of the homes that once lined the streets of the Gramercy Park neighborhood with their heavy window enframements and wood cornices that are usually supported by curving brackets.

In about 1913, journalist, muckraker and author Ida Tarbell (1857–1954) moved into a modest apartment in this row house, and she could have been seen in and about the Gramercy neighborhood until she moved in 1940. Tarbell had already written "The History of Standard Oil" in 1902. It was originally published in *McClure's Magazine*, serialized in nineteen parts, and then published in a two-volume hardcover set and followed by an abridged paperback edition. The book exposed corrupt practices of John D.

Rockefeller and Standard Oil in its climb to dominate America's oil industry and is credited with inspiring a number of others to write about corrupt big businesses and robber barons. It wasn't long after the books about Rockefeller were published that the U.S. government brought conspiracy charges (under the Sherman Anti-Trust Act) against Standard Oil, and the company was broken up into thirty-four smaller companies.

Tarbell wrote over a dozen books, including works about individuals such as Abraham Lincoln, Napoleon Bonaparte and Madame Roland. In her book *Tariff in Our Times*, concerning the financial history of the United States, she describes examples of how one tariff after another failed to accomplish what they were supposed to and reveals the selfish motives of their advocates. Tarbell gradually became distrustful of politics—so much so that she refused President Woodrow Wilson's offer to appoint her tariff commissioner. She questioned the cause of women's suffrage and militant feminism in her 1912 autobiography *The Business of Being a Woman*. While Tarbell wrote favorably about scientific management planner Frederick W. Taylor, she also strongly endorsed the idea that the way to gain better productivity in factories was through the good treatment of their workers. And Tarbell wrote that female factory managers would be as capable as men (she never really addressed the contradiction in her aforementioned writing and her stated views about a woman's place being in the home and her apparent opposition to women's suffrage). Despite any seeming inconsistency in her ideas, Tarbell's lifetime of writing, whether her journalism or her books, gives a detailed factual record of the issues and conditions that existed during the late nineteenth and early twentieth centuries.

If we walk on East Nineteenth Street toward Park Avenue South, we will come to 119 East Nineteenth Street. The National Arts Club Studio Building opened in 1906 as a cooperative with studios for artists to live and work in. It was designed by the well-known architect George B. Post, a fifteen-story building with a brick-and-limestone façade sporting tiny gargoyles over the entrance and terra-cotta plaques with NAC (National Arts Club) over the gargoyles. The building has been converted to a rental owned by—and located directly behind—the National Arts Club (15 Gramercy Park South).

In 1906, journalist, novelist and muckraker David Graham Phillips (1867–1911) moved into an apartment in the National Arts Club Studio Building with his sister Mrs. Caroline Frevert (divorced). H.L. Mencken called Phillips "the leading American novelist," and in 1911, the newspapers reported his murder as the "Literary Murder of the Twentieth Century." Phillips was born in Madison, Indiana; graduated college; worked as a reporter in Cincinnati,

David Graham Phillips. *Courtesy of the Library of Congress.*

Ohio; and then moved to New York in about 1890. As a journalist, his stories were about big business (Standard Oil) and how it corrupted the U.S. Senate. It was Phillips's investigative reporting (known as "muckraking") that caused the U.S. senators from New York, Chauncey M. Depew and Thomas C. Platt, to resign. Phillips can be credited with inspiring other writers such as Lincoln Steffens and Upton Sinclair, who became much better known for exposing government corruption. And even over fifty years later, it is interesting to note the similarities between Tom Wolfe and Phillips. Both were sharp social critics; both were flamboyant, wearing white suits as journalists in the newsrooms; and both used their popularity to foster their literary careers as novelists. Tom Wolfe became known for his influence over the New Journalism literary movement, and Phillips pioneered muckraking (investigative reporting). And even in his novels, Phillips combined romance stories with the corruption rampant in the worlds of finance, insurance and politics.

By 1911, Phillips had written several novels: *The Grain of Dust, The Great God Success, The Plum Tree, The Price She Paid, The Second Generation, Susan Lenox: Her Fall and Rise, The Conflict, The Cost* and *The Deluge.* But you could say, as did Peter Duffy in his essay for the *New York Times Book Review* on January 14, 2011, that it was Phillips's novel *The Fashionable Adventures of Joshua Craig,* published in 1909, that resulted in his deadliest book review.

From a prominent Maryland family, Fitzhugh Coyle Goldsborough—a Harvard-educated violinist and a first chair violinist for the Pittsburgh Symphony Orchestra from 1907 to 1909—believed that Phillips's novel *The Fashionable Adventures of Joshua Craig* referred to and cast aspersions against his family, especially his younger sister.

David Phillips rose late on Monday, January 23, 1911. He had been working the night before on the corrective proofs of his new short story, "Susan Lenox: Her Fall and Rise," which was later published posthumously as a novel. Phillips was carrying the final proofs that he intended to mail to the *Saturday Evening Post* magazine as he took the elevator to the first floor of his building and continued on the street walking around Gramercy Park, heading for his daily stop at the Princeton Club. Fitzhugh Coyle Goldsborough confronted Phillips near the club's entrance and yelled, "Here you go," and rapidly shot him six times. Then Goldsborough yelled, "Here I go," and fatally shot himself in the head. David Graham Phillips died the next day in Bellevue Hospital—but not before stating that he never knew or heard of Fitzhugh Coyle Goldsborough or of the Goldsborough family and that they had absolutely nothing to do with his novel.

In the 1992 novel *The Seventh Bullet*, by Daniel D. Victor, Sherlock Holmes investigates the Phillips murder.

This is the only building on this block that is part of the Gramercy Park Historic District, but there are several other buildings on the block that are noteworthy and have been proposed by the Gramercy Neighborhood Associates Inc. as an extension to the Gramercy Park Historic District. If we look at 117 and 115 East Nineteenth Street, we will see two narrow, four-story Anglo-Italianate brownstone-fronted homes with mansard roofs that were built about 1853. They still have some of the original wood window sash and iron railings. Then we continue west to 113 and 111 East Nineteenth Street, erected about 1855. These two houses were built by Judge Thomas J. Oakley, and his home at 12 Gramercy Park South backed up to these lots on East Nineteenth Street. The two houses retain their original ground-floor arcade, segmental-arched windows and wooden cornices. From 1906 to 1911, 113 East Nineteenth Street was home to Henry Herts (1871–1933), and his architectural firm Herts & Tallant was also located in the building. Herts & Tallant are best remembered for their design of such theaters as the New Amsterdam, Lyceum and Brooklyn Academy of Music. The interior details that were original to the two houses reflected the taste of the architects and, to some extent, are still apparent.

No. 109 East Nineteenth Street is a row house with a brownstone Anglo-Italianate front, built in 1896 by Elihu Townsend, a banker who financed several such row houses in the neighborhood. Designed by Herts & Tallant with round arch ground-floor openings, iron railings, parlor floor casement windows and a deep cornice over paired brackets. There was a one-story addition in the back in 1908, and in 1932, the upper floors were converted into six apartments.

In 1985, Nicholas Pileggi was living here when he wrote the book *Wise Guy: Life in a Mafia Family*, and in the early 1990s, it was in this row house that Pileggi and Martin Scorsese wrote the screenplay *Goodfellas* based on the book.

No. 105 East Nineteenth Street was designed by architects Neville & Bagge and is a six-story Neo-Renaissance apartment building with a rusticated limestone base and brick upper floors. The façade is trimmed with terra-cotta detail and has a metal cornice on top. The apartment building opened in 1896 with two eight-room apartments on each floor.

On the south side of the street, 108 East Nineteenth Street was originally the Interborough Rapid Transit Co. Substation. After many years of planning and discussion, work finally began in 1899 on the construction of the Interborough Rapid Transit (IRT), New York's first subway line. Electricity was generated at an enormous power plant located between Eleventh and Twelfth Avenues and West Fifty-eight and West Fifty-ninth Streets. The coal-burning power plant generated alternating current, which was directed to eight substations located along the route of the subway line, where it was converted into direct current, which then flowed into the third rail on the subway tracks.

This powerhouse opened in 1904 and was designed by John Van Vleck and Paul C. Hunter. It is an eclectic four-story structure, and the façade's massing is reminiscent of an Italian Renaissance palazzo. It displays French Beaux-Arts details, such as cartouches and brackets hung with garlands. The façade has a granite base, limestone midsection and an upper story faced with brick laid in a Georgian-inspired Flemish-bond pattern with burned headers. The building also has iron window bays and terra-cotta detail and is no longer used as a power station. The vacant building was cleaned between 1990 and 1991.

The reason the power station's façade resembles that of a mansion is because the city contract allowing the Interborough Rapid Transit Co. to construct the subway system stated in part: "The railway and its equipment as contemplated by the contract constitute a great public work. All parts of the structure where exposed to public sight shall therefore be designed, constructed, and maintained with a view to the beauty of their appearance, as well as to their efficiency."

We will walk back past Irving Place to the Block Beautiful, which is East Nineteenth Street between Irving Place and Third Avenue.

Chapter 5

THE BLOCK BEAUTIFUL

AN ARTIST COLONY

B lock Beautiful got its nickname in 1914 when Harriet Gillespie used the phrase to describe the block in *American Homes and Gardens* magazine, and it stuck. In the 1840s and '50s, this block was developed with brick and brownstone row houses for well-to-do New Yorkers. But by 1900, the block was sliding into middle- and working-class housing. In 1906, Frederick Sterner purchased 139 East Nineteenth Street and gave it his signature remodeling, removing the stoop and using colored stucco on its façade. In 1911, banker and polo player Joseph B. Thomas hired Frederick Sterner to remodel 132 and 135 East Nineteenth Street in the same style. Then a number of homeowners on the block hired Sterner to remodel their buildings, and others just followed his example, thus creating what became known as "Block Beautiful." Sterner believed that the interior living space should be primary and the exterior should complement the interior, so in many of the homes he remodeled, the dull Victorian interiors were redesigned in a manner even more stunning than the exterior.

Frederick Sterner moved to East Sixty-fifth Street in 1915 and to London, England, in 1924.

By the 1920s and into the 1930s, the block was attracting an informal colony of artists and writers that included author Ida Tarbell, painter Cecilia Beaux and sculptor George Julian Zolnay. Also living here at the time was music critic and novelist Carl Van Vechten and the well-known painters George Bellows and Robert Chanler. Van Vechten and others on the block became well known for their wild parties, about which Ethel Barrymore

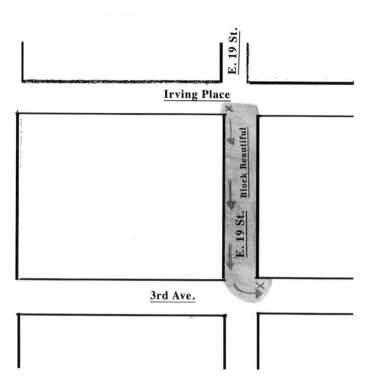

Map of Block Beautiful.

commented, "I went there in the evening a young girl and came away in the morning an old woman."

In 1921, Helen Lowery, a reporter working for the *New York Times*, credited Sterner with the idea of the picturesque "Italian" front (Sterner's Mediterranean style) and with the idea of reviving older neighborhoods for upper-class residents. By then, redevelopment had taken place at Turtle Bay Gardens (East Forty-ninth Street between Second and Third Avenues) and at Sutton Place (East Fifty-third Street to East Fifty-ninth Street).

As we walk east on East Nineteenth Street toward Third Avenue, we will pass 124 East Nineteenth Street. It is a former carriage house with great Dutch-style stepped gables. In 1866, James C. Clinch lived in a brownstone home at 124 East Nineteenth Street. At the time, the block was lined with similar houses, all home to respectable merchant-class families. But only a few decades later, the house was replaced by a quaint, one-story carriage house that reflected an interest in the city's Dutch roots, with a brick stepped gable and a shallow, dentil-molded cornice.

With the turn of the century came the automobile and a car dealer, R. Bertelli & Co., which used 124 East Nineteenth Street as its headquarters for the sale of the Zust, an Italian automobile named for its maker, Robert Zust. Bertelli introduced the high-end car at the Sixty-Ninth Regiment Armory automobile show in 1905 and announced on New Year's Eve that it was the sole sales agent for the car. The *New York Times* noted that the car "has many points to commend it" and "has won many contests in Europe, including a hill-climbing contest from Milan to Florence, when Robert Zust, driving a forty-fifty horse power car, was the only one to finish."

We continue to walk a bit to 128 East Nineteenth Street. This house was built between 1830 and 1840 as a carriage house three stories high, and later, at the turn of the last century, it was rebuilt for residential use. From 1953 to 1996, it was home to Lincoln Kirstein (born 1907 in Rochester, New York, and died in 1996 in Manhattan). He referred to it as his "midget mansion." The home had 4,370 square feet of interior space, with three bedrooms, four and a half baths and a large terrace on top of a ballroom, and he had a grand piano on the ground floor for entertaining. There is a nice relatively new Art Modern iron fence, along with a commemorative plaque for Kirstein in front.

Kirstein's father was a department store magnate and vice-president of Filene's in Boston (one opened in Manhattan in the 1990s), and he set up a trust fund that allowed Kirstein to follow his passion for the arts, which was evident even from the time he spent at Harvard working on his bachelor's degree. As a student in the 1930s, Kirstein started the literary magazine *House & Horn* and then formed the Harvard Society for Contemporary Art, which became a forerunner to the Museum of Modern Art in Manhattan. To say that he was an art patron and an important figure in the art world seems as a bit of an understatement when we remember that in 1933 Kirstein invited George Balanchine (the Russian dancer and choreographer) to New York City, and they formed the School of American Ballet and several other ballet companies, along with the New York City Ballet, of which Kirstein was its general director from 1946 to 1989. Lincoln Kirstein wrote thirty books, including *Dance*, which was an account of his partnership with Balanchine. In 1941, he married Fidelma Cadmus (sister of the artist Paul Cadmus). Kirstein was involved in any number of relationships, and in his later years, he struggled with paranoia, manic depression and bipolar disorder.

In 1997, George Wolfe (born 1954) paid $1.75 million for 128 East Nineteenth Street. George Wolfe is a playwright, producer and director of theater and film. He is a suitable successor for Kirstein's midget mansion as his continuing artistic achievements are contributing to the neighborhood's artistic legacy. Wolfe first gained his national reputation with his 1991 musical *Jelly's Last Jam*, a musical about the life of jazz musician Jelly Roll Morton. The Broadway play received eleven Tony nominations, and Wolfe won the Drama Desk Award for Outstanding Book of a Musical. From 1993 to 2004, Wolfe was artistic director and producer for Joseph Papp's New York Shakespeare Festival/Public Theater (on Lafayette Place). In 1993, he won a Tony for directing *Angels in America: Millennium Approaches* and won a Tony again in 1996 for directing *Bring in da Noise/Bring in da Funk*. George Wolfe was inducted into the American Theater Hall of Fame in 2013, and his artistic works continue to the present day.

Across the street at 127–129 East Nineteenth Street, in 1861, two two-story stables were built on this site. One was used by an iron merchant, James Cooper Lord, who lived in his townhouse at 24 Gramercy Park South. By the early 1890s, both stables were converted for use as studio spaces for Craige F.R. Drake, a master stained-glass blower.

In 1903, F. Berkeley Smith purchased 129 East Nineteenth Street and had its exterior and interior remodeled into a single-family residence with two bedrooms, fireplaces and wood paneling, along with a boudoir for his wife and a trunk-room, all with wood wainscoting, antique metal lamps, artwork and other artistic touches. It was probably this remodeling in 1903 that gave the house its Gothic Revival gingerbread detail, and it was later in the same year that the *New York Times* described 129 East Nineteenth Street as possessing the most "picturesque exterior" in all of Manhattan.

F. Berkeley Smith (1869–1931) was the son of the successful author Francis Hopkinson Smith and worked as an author and artist. Berkeley's use of the house was limited since he traveled a great deal and spent his summers in Paris, France. Throughout the twentieth century, the house had several owners. And by 1997, both structures were combined into one house (with 1,800 square feet of interior space) simulating some of the Gothic styled features of its predecessors.

No. 135 East Nineteenth Street was built in 1845. By 1910, the plain Greek Revival home was owned by Joseph B. Thomas, who hired Frederick Sterner to redesign it into a picturesque-style home that some called a "Gothic fantasy," while others described the house as having a Mediterranean style. Sterner slathered it with colored stucco and added a Mediterranean-style red tile roof that extended beyond the façade, and he used colorful tiles and decorative ironwork to accentuate the design. He also created a below-street-level entrance and a stone first floor that supports four stories of multicolored modified Flemish bond brick work, along with diamond-paned windows that are topped by flat-headed Gothic eyebrows throughout the façade. Stained glass windows and carved tracery mark the dinning room floor. On top is a stepped gable with crouching gargoyles and a carved coat of arms that reflect the Gothic motif. Frederick Sterner changed an outmoded house into an up-to-date and eye-catching home for Thomas.

Oleg Cassini (born Oleg Aleksandrovich Loiewski), a prestigious American fashion designer, was living here at 135 East Nineteenth Street and in Oyster Bay, New York, at the time of his death. Oleg Cassini (1913–2006) was born in Paris, raised in Italy and moved to the United States in 1936. Cassini designed clothes for various Hollywood studios and during World War II was a second lieutenant in the United States Army. After the war, in New York, he designed ready-to-wear dresses and costumes for television and Broadway.

Cassini's first wife (1938–41) was cough-syrup heiress Merry Fahrney. He married his second wife, actress Gene Tierney, in 1941. Tierney's parents didn't approve, so the couple eloped to Las Vegas and used earrings as wedding rings. They had two daughters, Antoinette Daria (who was deaf, blind and developmentally disabled) and Christine "Tina" Cassini. Tierney had an affair with John F. Kennedy, and the couple divorced in 1952. At one time, Cassini was engaged to Grace Kelly. In 1960s, Jacqueline Kennedy chose him to design her state wardrobe. Oleg Cassini wrote his autobiography *In My Own Style* in 1987, and he died in 2006. He is survived by his third wife, Marianne; his two children; and four grandchildren. Cassini's property in Oyster Bay, New York, was once part of the estate of Louis Comfort Tiffany.

On the south side of the street is 132 East Nineteenth Street, an apartment house that was built about 1850 and remodeled between 1906 and 1911 by Frederick Sterner in a dramatic half-timbered style using tinted stucco and shutters on the façade, along with decorative iron work and a projecting tile roof. He used old brick and polychrome tile panels to give an informal handmade appearance (note the tile work around the doorway and the tile platters).

At different points in time, this apartment house has been home to actress Theda Bara; society painter Cecilia Beaux; stock broker Chester Dale, who started his great art collection here; and painter and muralist Albert Sterner, Frederick Sterner's brother.

Theda Bara was one of the most successful and glamorous stars of the 1910s, behind only Mary Pickford and Charlie Chaplin in popularity. She made forty-four films, most of them between 1914 and 1919, and of all films she made from 1914 to 1926, only three and a half remain. The facts of her life were jumbled by studio publicity, and even her birth date and place were obscure. She was responsible for the word "vamp" being created and used to describe a seductive woman. According to her studio's publicity, Theda Bara was born in the shadow of the Pyramids, the daughter of an Italian artist and a French actress. Everyone knew it was nonsense; the stories were never meant to be taken seriously. Film history books state that Bara was born 1890, in Cincinnati, Ohio. Actually, Theodosia Goodman (as she was named at birth) was really born in Avondale (a wealthy, largely Jewish, suburb of Cincinnati) in 1885.

Unlike her public image would suggest, Theda was an alert intellectual. She went to college for two years and was a voracious reader all of her life. She preferred books that dealt with philosophy and psychology. Theda dropped out of college in 1905 to pursue an acting career in Manhattan and tried unsuccessfully for ten years to become a stage actress. She was pushing thirty when director Frank Powell cast her as the vampire in William Fox's film version of the Broadway hit *A Fool There Was* in 1915. She was an instant star, saving the fortunes of the fledgling Fox Studios. Theda had been a rather solemn and pretentious teenager, but she was a cooperative and good-natured star, going along with all the studio publicity hype. Fox Studios created her family history for each film role, and she played along. Dressed in veils, furs and silks and even petting a python and nibbling on raw beef, she deadpanned her way through hundreds of ludicrous press conferences. And for the most part, reporters played along and printed interviews with straight faces.

The only thing that frustrated Theda was that in her screen roles, she was always cast as an unrepentant vamp bent on wholesale destruction. She fought for better roles and sometimes got them. Her personal favorites were her role as a heroic Foreign Legion girl in *Under Two Flags* and her performance as an innocent Irish peasant girl in *Kathleen Mavourneen*. She also played some of the great heroines of history and literature, including Cleopatra, Salome, Carmen, Juliet, Madame DuBarry and Marguerite Gautier—all in all, not a bad career.

Theda was smart enough to save her money and enjoy the moment. In 1917, her movie studio forced her to move to California, but she never got used to the West Coast, with its lack of museums, bookstores, theaters and decent shops. And for over thirty-seven years, right up to the end of her life, Theda kept her apartment on East Nineteenth Street furnished and ready for trips. She also sublet the apartment to other actresses and friends, including Mrs. Patrick Campbell. By the time America entered World War I, Theda was the third-biggest star in the nation. She joined the war effort with great enthusiasm, visiting camps, raising hundreds of thousands of dollars in War Bonds and contributing her salary to charity. Songs were written about Theda, and postcards and magazines featuring her face sold briskly. Dangling earrings, kohled eyes, languorous glances and the catchy line, "Kiss me, my fool!" entered the public consciousness.

In 1921, she married successful movie director Charles Brabin, a marriage that lasted until her death. The Brabins were wealthy globe-trotters, and Theda's skills as a hostess and gourmet cook made their Beverly Hills home a favorite stopping place for the film community through the 1950s. Her one regret was that Brabin did not want her to act (she made two films in the mid-1920s while he was in Italy directing a movie).

The famous English actress Mrs. Patrick Campbell (1865–1940) sublet Theda Bara's apartment in 1927; it was Campbell who had originated the Eliza Doolittle role in *Pygmalion* written for her by George Bernard Shaw. The first time it was presented on a New York stage was at the Park Theater that was located on Columbus Circle at the time.

Mrs. Patrick Campbell made her debut in 1888, and her first London success was in 1892 in the title role of Pinero's *Second Mrs. Tanquery*. She became the most successful British stage actress of her generation. Her maiden name was Beatrice Stella Tanner of Kennsington, London. Her mother was Italian, and her father was English. In 1914, fourteen years after her first husband died, she became the second wife of George Cornwallis-West (born 1874), a dashing writer previously married to Jennie Jerome, the mother of Winston Churchill, but she continued to use Mrs. Patrick Campbell as her stage name. She is remembered for her great beauty and wit and her long association with George Bernard Shaw.

In 1901, she made the first of her many tours to the United States. In 1912, she met George Bernard Shaw, at whose request she originated the role of Eliza Doolittle in *Pygmalion* (supposedly he wrote the play for her). Even though she was too old for the part at forty-nine, she was the obvious choice, being by far the biggest name on the London stage.

Mrs. Patrick Campbell made a number of memorable appearances on American stage, which she describes in her 1922 autobiography, *My Life and Some Letters.* In the latter part of her life, Campbell made a number of appearances in American movies. She died in France.

As we continue walking east, at 141 East Nineteenth Street, we see a jockey hitching post at the doorway marking the home of Edward "Ted" Brit Husing (1891–1962), a famous sportscaster who was inducted into the American Broadcaster's Association (ABA) Hall of Fame in 1984. The foremost sports announcer, he was largely responsible for play-by-play broadcasting as we know it. Husing's ability to capture the drama of sports as it was played helped advance sportscasting to the exciting medium that it is today.

Husing began broadcasting in 1925 for RCA-WJZ and worked with various networks, including CBS and ABC. His style—concise and crystal clear, with a smooth delivery and an easy speaking manner—made many a dull game interesting, making him a favorite with the audience and ensuring his lasting success. Husing enjoyed his celebrity standing and made the 21 Club his unofficial headquarters. In the late 1950s, he had an operation for a brain tumor and went blind. He subsequently moved to California, where his mother and daughter took care of him.

No. 145 East Nineteenth Street was built in 1843 in a mundane Greek Revival style. It was remodeled by Frederick Sterner in 1911.

The next building at 147–149 East Nineteenth Street has two addresses and ceramic reliefs with images of giraffes with intertwined necks over each of its entrances. The reliefs were created by the resident artist Robert Winthrop Chanler (1872–1930), who moved here in the early 1900s and created this as his "House of Fantasy" by decorating with his own works. Chanler was a well-known painter and muralist who was involved in the Paris art community of the 1890s. When he moved here, he became a personality and a figure in his time and made 147–149 East Nineteenth Street his home and work studio, as well as a central social gathering location for New York's art community. Chanler created the giraffe mosaics over his doorways because they represented his best-known work *Giraffes,* which was created in 1905 and later purchased by the French government. Although Chanler was sometimes referred to as eccentric and almost bizarre, his works were well received. There are murals of his that are still prominent, such as a ceiling mural of buffaloes in the Coe House in Brookville, New York, and a ceiling mural inside the Colony Club on Park Avenue and Sixty-second Street in Manhattan.

Robert Winthrop Chanler was born to a wealthy New York Hudson River family who were related to the Astor, Delano, Winthrop and Stuyvesant

One entrance to 147–149 East Nineteenth Street, Robert W. Chanler's home.

families. He studied in France at the Ecole des Beaux-Arts and was a close friend of Gertrude Vanderbilt Whitney, founder of the Whitney Museum. Chanler decorated Gertrude's studio, which was in the rear yard of today's New York Studio School of Drawing, Painting and Sculpture at 12 West Eighth Street (the first building to house the Whitney Museum in the 1930s), with cobalt blue windows depicting bats, fish and dragons amid seaweed and constellations. Chanler specialized in painted screens and was a member of the National Society of Mural Painters. He was also a member of the New York Architectural League and was featured in the 1913 New York Armory Show.

Across East Nineteenth Street from Chanler's home is 146 East Nineteenth Street, and on the façade is a plaque saying that this was the home of George Bellows (1883–1925). He had just married his wife, Emma, in 1910 when they purchased and moved into this house. His painting studio was on the third floor, with the windows facing the northern light. George lived here with Emma and his two daughters: Ann, born in 1911, and Jean, born in 1915. He used to take his young daughters to play in Gramercy Park until he died in 1925 from a ruptured appendix at forty-two years old.

George Bellows was a late disciple of the Ashcan School (New York Realist), an important movement that evolved in the early twentieth century. Members of this movement included a diverse group of painters

Above: No. 146 East Nineteenth Street was home to George Bellows.

Left: Self-portrait of George Bellows. *Courtesy of the Library of Congress.*

with a core group of eight: George Luks, Robert Henri, Arthur B. Davies, Maurice Prendergast, Ernest Lawson, William Glackens, Everett Shinn and John Sloan. They opposed academies and had their first public exhibit at Macbeth Gallery in 1908. They were reviled by some critics as "the revolutionary black gang" and the "apostles of ugliness." Another critic said that their work belonged in the ashcan, so they decided to adopt the Ashcan School as their name.

These artists played a role in founding the Society of Independent Artists in 1917. They were conservative in style but revolutionary in content, focusing on urban scenes, especially those in the shabbier parts of city life, and portraying urban vitality. Four of the painters started as newspaper illustrators, and their work introduced a gritty realism and informality with such paintings as *The Wrestlers*, *The Shoppers*, *Hairdressers Window* and *Sixth Avenue*.

Not many of George Bellows's friends had children, especially in the rebellious group known as the "Washington Square Crowd," in which almost all were passionately against the United States entering World War I. Even though George Bellows shared their view for a long time, in April 1917, when President Woodrow Wilson finally asked Congress for a Declaration of War, Bellows supported the need to defend democracy. Terrible stories coming from Europe influenced him. In an article he wrote for a journal called *Touchstone*, he explained, "I would enlist in any army to make the world more beautiful. I would go to war for an idea far more easily than I would go for a country. Democracy to me is the Big Idea."

He also supported the rights of others to oppose war. Columnists for the Communist newspaper the *Masses* and its editors were all friends of Bellows, and they were indicted under the Espionage Act.

At the northwest corner of Third Avenue, at 151 East Nineteenth Street, is an apartment building where Carl Van Vechten (1880–1964) moved into a small apartment in 1932 with his second wife, Fania Marinoff. Carl Van Vechten was a multitalented writer who worked as a drama and music critic and who wrote novels. He also pursued a career as a photographer and is probably best remembered as a chronicler of the Harlem Renaissance between 1918 and 1929. Van Vechten also was a friend, a host and an appreciative audience to three generations of celebrities in the arts, literature and society.

Van Vechten was born and raised in Cedar Rapids, Iowa, by older parents who encouraged his interest in music, literature and writing. He graduated from the University of Chicago in 1903 and moved to Manhattan in 1906 and was hired as the assistant music critic for the *New York Times*. In 1913, Van

Carl van Vechten. *Courtesy of the Library of Congress.*

Vechten became the literary executor of Gertrude Stein's estate and aided in publishing her unpublished works. While working for the *New York Times*, he became the first American critic of modern dance, writing about the performances of Isadora Duncan, Anna Pavlova and Loie Fuller.

Van Vechten came from Cedar Falls, but while living in Manhattan, he cut a distinctive figure riding around town on his new bicycle and dressed with large shoulder pads in his jacket, tight pants, an ascot, patent leather shoes and a derby hat and one very long fingernail.

Chapter 6

ACTORS AND FAMOUS
HISTORICAL FIGURES

GRAMERCY PARK SOUTH TO IRVING PLACE

Now, we leave East Nineteenth Street, making a left on Third Avenue and then another left turn on to East Twentieth Street. As we walk west and pass by 32 Gramercy Park South and look up to our left, we will see the rear of 147–149 East Nineteenth Street displaying its large top-floor studio windows, which allowed Robert Chanler to take advantage of the well-known northern light for his studio.

And as we continue to walk, we will quickly come upon 144 East Twentieth Street (28 Gramercy Park South), originally built as Friends Meeting House in 1859 for Hicksite Quakers. The architects were King & Kellum, and the firm created an austere Anglo-Italianate (sometimes mistakenly referred to as Greek Revival) meetinghouse for the Quakers, who stayed here until 1958, when they reunited with another group of Quakers on Rutherford Place, only several blocks from here.

The Brotherhood Synagogue paid $420,000 for the building, which was renovated and restored in 1974 by architect James Polshek. Both Polshek and the contractor, Lawrence Held and Son, donated their services. The sensitive restoration cost about $300,000, and the building is a New York City landmark. In the words of the architectural critic and historian Anna Louise Huxtable, "The building...meets a universal need to touch base with the past, to savor timeless esthetic excellence, to enjoy an essential and enriching aspect of New York life. In art and amenity, it is beyond price."

The gardens on both sides of the synagogue are 1974 additions: on the east side is the Garden of Remembrance, with a limestone wall engraved

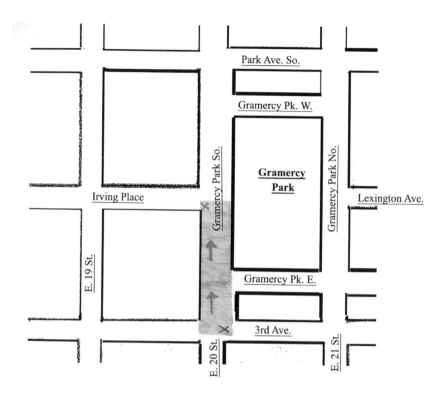

Map of Gramercy Park South.

Brotherhood Synagogue, at 28 Gramercy Park South (Friends Meeting House).

with the names of Holocaust victims and members of the congregation who have died. The garden on the west side, the Biblical Gardens, has a memorial mosaic on the far end symbolizing the synagogue's goal of peace.

At the southeast corner of Gramercy Park and the northeast corner of Gramercy Park South and Gramercy Park East there is 34 Gramercy Park East, the Gramercy Apartment House, which opened in 1883 as Manhattan's first luxury cooperative apartment building. It was designed by George Da Cunha, the same architect who gave us the first Plaza Hotel. The nine-story red brick building with a brownstone base, terra-cotta detail and great Queen Anne forms is sometimes described as Victorian or Renaissance Revival in style. The façade features an octagonal turret corner, lion heads over the entrance, Indian faces on the third floor, eagle heads on the fourth floor and geometric squares on the sixth and seventh floors. The otter lobby tile floor gives the impression of being a mosaic, but it isn't because the designs are in the tiles themselves rather than the tiles making up the design. The inner lobby has English encaustic tile floors. The building retained and used its great birdcage elevators from 1883 until they were replaced in the 1990s.

Jimmy Fallon (born 1974), host of NBC's *The Tonight Show Starring Jimmy Fallon*, bought his first unit in the Gramercy in 2002, on the seventh floor. As of 2014, he has five units in the building. Fallon's *Tonight Show* is now filmed in Manhattan, where the show first appeared over fifty-two years ago with Johnny Carson (before the show moved to California in 1972). The show's return to 30 Rockefeller Plaza brings over one hundred jobs to New York and gives tourists another reason to visit our city.

Over 120-some odd years ago, in the 1890s, the first celebrity moved into 34 Gramercy Park East: Emma Thursby (1845–1931), a world renowned concert singer. She was born and raised in Brooklyn and began singing with a Dutch Reform Church. By 1857, Emma was studying music at the Bethlehem Female Seminary with Sylvester and Francis Wolle. In the 1870s, Emma was performing to acclaim in concerts with Patrick Gilmore's Twenty-second Regiment Band, and her venues included the Philadelphia Academy of Music. Before long, she signed a contract with Maurice Strakosch for $100,000 for a tour across North America, and later she was performing in London, France and Germany. In 1881, Thursby was the first American awarded the medal of the Societe des Concerts of the Paris Conservatory. Emma Thursby was the first American woman to have an international musical career and America's most popular female singer at the time. When she was thirty-nine years old, her mother and sister passed away, and Emma performed much less frequently.

Left: No. 34 Gramercy Park East, Gramercy Entrance.

Below: Gramercy Park Southeast corner (the Gramercy). *Original watercolor by Ann Woodward.*

She taught as a professor of music at the Institute of Musical Art (now Julliard School) in Manhattan and held weekly salons every Friday at her Gramercy apartment, which became widely known as Thursby's Fridays. The current topics of the day were discussed by important figures in politics, along with writers, journalists, newspaper publishers and celebrities of the day. It was much coveted to be invited to Thursby's Fridays. Emma Thursby died in her apartment at the Gramercy in 1931 at the age of eighty-six. Her papers are held by the New York Historical Society.

Other residents here over the years included Mildred Dunnock (1901–1991), a stage and movie character actress who won an Oscar in 1951 (best supporting actress) for *Death of a Salesman*. Margaret Hamilton (1902–1985) was the Wicked Witch of the West in *The Wizard of Oz* and appeared in seventy-five movies, seventy plays and seven television films. Jimmy Cagney (1899–1986) was an actor on stage and in movies who starred in over sixty films and was a dancer early in his career. Cagney was born and raised on Manhattan's Lower East Side, and he graduated Stuyvesant High School and attended Columbia College. He worked several different jobs before getting his start in vaudeville as a "song and dance man" (comedian). Cagney's first non-dancing role in a play was in 1925 in *Outside Looking In*. He got several more roles, receiving good notices, and then in 1929 got the lead in the play *Penny Arcade*—his ticket to Hollywood. Cagney got rave reviews, and Warner Bros. signed him to a $500-a-week, three-week contract to reprise his role. This soon was changed to a seven-year contract. Cagney had an apartment here for two years.

John Carradine (1906–1988) was a protégé and close friend of John Barrymore. Carradine was an extremely prolific movie character actor and also had a career as a stage actor with leading classic roles. In later years, he starred in a number of horror movies and was a member of John Ford's Stock Company. He was married four times, and three of his sons—David, Keith and Robert—have acting careers.

As we continue west, almost immediately we will come to 26 Gramercy Park South, built as the Hotel Irving in 1903 (converted to co-ops in 1983). This is the site where the acclaimed novelist and dramatist Booth Tarkington (1869–1946) lived while he was in Manhattan. Tarkington won the Pulitzer Prize for *The Magnificent Ambersons* in 1918 and again for *Alice Adams* in 1922. He was born in Indianapolis, and his most popular works were genial novels of life in small Midwestern towns, including *The Gentleman from Indiana* (1899) and *The Conquest of Canaan* (1905). Some of his best work depicts the frustrated ambitions of a romantic lower-middle-class girl. He wrote several amusing novels about boyhood and adolescence, including *Penrod* (1914) and *Seventeen* (1916). His plays include a dramatization of his own historical romance *Monsieur Beaucaire* (1901) and *Clarence* (1921). Ludwig Bemelmans (chapter 3) also stayed at the Hotel Irving.

The building at 24 Gramercy Park South opened in 1909 and converted to co-ops in 1956. Inventor Thomas Edison (1847–1931) was thirty-four years old when he rented an apartment in a building that was at 24 Gramercy Park South (the original building was demolished in 1908). Edison was doing well by this time and lived here in 1880 and 1881 with his wife, Mary, and their young daughter Marion before moving to New Jersey. When Edison first came to Manhattan by himself seeking opportunities in the 1870s, there was a depression going on (lasting until 1878), and he couldn't find a job. After three weeks in Manhattan, Edison was on the verge of starving. He was wandering through some offices in the financial district when he saw that a local brokerage firm was in a panic because no one in the office could fix an important broken stock ticker. Edison took the opportunity to fix it. Luckily, he had been sleeping in the building's basement for a few days and snooping around, so he was already familiar with the device. Edison reached down and moved a loose spring back to where it belonged. The device ran perfectly. The office manager was ecstatic and hired Edison on the spot to make such repairs for the busy company for a salary of $300 a month, which was twice the going rate for a top electrician in New York City. Later, Edison recalled that this was the most euphoric experience in his life because it made him feel that he had suddenly been delivered from abject poverty into prosperity. Edison resumed his "moonlighting" with the telegraph, the quadruplex transmitter, the stock ticker, etc. He nearly fainted when a corporation executive paid him $40,000 for the rights to his stock ticker device. He walked around for hours in a stupor of amazement. After he cashed the check, he laid the cash out on his bed and stayed up all night recounting it before depositing it in a bank. Edison continued creating successful inventions for industry and had several patents. In 1874, he opened his first complete testing and development laboratory in Newark, New Jersey.

The home at the site of 21 Gramercy Park South belonged to John Bigelow (1817–1911), co-owner of the *New York Post* from 1848 to 1861. During the Civil War, Bigelow sailed to France as our ambassador. He was able to convince the French government to stop its support for the Confederacy. Later, Bigelow was one of Samuel Tilden's estate trust executors and carried out Tilden's wishes to develop the New York Public Library, becoming one of the founders of and the first president of the library. Bigelow also was a strong supporter of the development of the Panama Canal and a friend of Philippe Bunau-Varilla, who brought Panama's Declaration of Independence to Bigelow's home.

Chapter 7

CLUB HOUSES AND MEMORIALS

Gramercy Park South to Park Avenue South

At the entrance to Gramercy Park at Irving Place is a plaque declaring it part of the Gramercy Park Historic District. At the center of Gramercy Park is a statue of Edwin Booth as Hamlet, dedicated and unveiled on November 13, 1918. Part of the collection of the trustees of Gramercy Park and a gift of the members of the Players Club, it was the work of sculptor Edmond T. Quinn (1868–1929).

The statue of Edwin Booth (1833–1893), depicted in his most famous role, holds his hands on his chest as he rises from a chair, readying himself for Hamlet's famous soliloquy, "To be or not to be." As a small, lithe, elegant figure with a magnificent voice, Edwin Booth captivated audiences with his stirring performances. He was regarded as America's greatest tragic stage actor.

Edwin Booth's *Hamlet* ran for one hundred nights at the Winter Garden Theater in 1864 in Manhattan—at a time when ten consecutive performances was considered a long run. His record lasted over fifty years and was broken by another resident of Gramercy Park, John Barrymore Jr., who lived at 36 Gramercy Park East. Edwin Booth's mansion is at 16 Gramercy Park South.

At the southeast corner of Irving Place and Gramercy Park South is 19 Gramercy Park South, built in 1845 for William S. Johnson, a Whig politician, and purchased in 1850 by Horace Brooks, a paper merchant, who added the Victorian mansard roof. It was remodeled as the Stuyvesant Fish mansion in 1887 by Stanford White of McKim, Mead & White and/or by Sidney V. Stratton, as a Federal-style mansion for Stuyvesant and Mamie Fish.

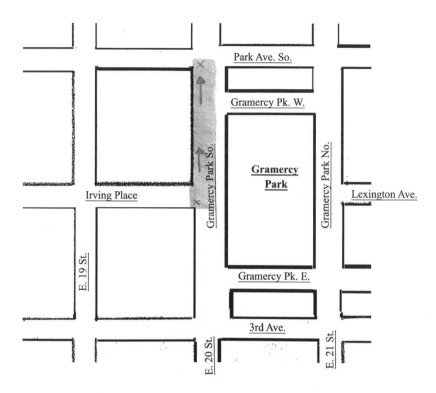

Map of Gramercy Park South.

Statue of Edwin Booth as Hamlet in the center of Gramercy Park.

No. 19 Gramercy Park South, the Stuyvesant Fish Mansion (with chimneys), and an adjacent apartment house.

Sidney V. Stratton (1845–1921) was one of the first American students at the Eçole des Beaux-Arts in Paris, along with H.H. Richardson and Richard Morris Hunt. Stratton had worked for Hunt but went out on his own in the 1870s. He met Charles McKim in France and sublet space from McKim, Mead & White in 1877. They developed an unusual arrangement that lasted until 1889. Stratton was listed on the firm's letterhead, underneath the partners' names and separated from them by a line. He was very well connected to New York society and may have helped the firm, especially in the beginning of their relationship, to gain access to that world, but they pursued and designed jobs independently. But this does not necessarily exclude collaboration on some projects. Samuel G. White, great-grandson of Sanford White and a partner at Buttrick White & Burtis and author of *The Houses of McKim, Mead & White* (Rizzoli, 1998) says, "The office was so small, everyone was working together." So it does seem to be a good chance of interior and exterior design collaboration on the Stuyvesant Fish mansion. In fact, Stratton collaborated with Stanford White on a church in Quogue, New York, and on the redesign of the Elliott Roosevelt town house in New York City in 1884.

Stuyvesant Fish (1851–1923) was a financier and a wealthy socialite. At the age of thirty-six, he was president of the Illinois Central Railroad, which had so many of New York's "400 Elite" on its board of directors that it was called the "Society Railroad." Stuyvesant Fish was the son of Hamilton Fish, a distinguished former New York governor and descendant of Peter Stuyvesant. There still stands a historic Stuyvesant Fish mansion on Stuyvesant Street in Manhattan that was Stuyvesant Fish's grandmother's home.

His wife, Marion "Mamie" Fish, followed Mrs. William B. Astor (Caroline Webster Schmerhorn) as the head of New York society in 1908. Mamie had a strong sense of humor and enjoyed playing practical jokes, especially on the "400 Elite." She encouraged more informality (by using first names) in society and shortened the traditional dinner hour from several hours to fifty minutes. Mamie and Stuyvesant Fish were childhood sweethearts who married and maintained a lifelong happy marriage. In 1900, they built and moved into a new mansion at 25 East Seventy-eighth Street along with a new country estate, Crosswinds in Newport, Rhode Island.

After 1900, the Stuyvesant Fish family leased the mansion to well-to-do merchant-class families. In 1909, an apartment building was constructed adjacent to the Stuyvesant Fish mansion, replacing an old stable, and the two buildings were managed by the Stuyvesant family as a high-end multi-dwelling complex, with tenants such as portrait artist Cecilia Beaux; famous actor John Barrymore; the infamous "Wolf of Wall Street," David Lamar; the playwright Edward Sheldon; and our ambassador to France in 1939, William C. Bullitt. In 1944, Norman Thomas (1884–1968) was living here when he was the Socialist Party candidate for president of the United States. Actually, he ran six times for president of the United States on the Socialist Party of America ticket and lost every time (see chapter 3).

In 1945, the high-profile publicist Benjamin Sonnenberg (1901–1978) paid $85,000 for both buildings and combined the mansion and the adjacent apartment house, creating eighteen thousand square feet of magnificent interiors. There are thirty-seven rooms that include thirteen fireplaces, six bedrooms and a dramatic ballroom. The vast private residence was sold in 1979, again in 1995 and finally in 2004 for $16.9 million to Dr. Henry Jarecki and his wife, Gloria, who planned to use it as a residence and a headquarters for their charitable trust, the Timber Falls Foundation. Dr. Jarecki is a clinical professor of psychiatry at Yale University School of Medicine.

No. 19 Gramercy Park South was the address of the boardinghouse in the 1970 novel *Time & Again* by Jack Finney, set in 1882. The character Simon Morley lived here, and his girlfriend from the past, Julia, worked here in her aunt's boardinghouse.

Now we'll look at the southwest corner of Irving Place and Gramercy Park South, and I'll give you a little background about the history of this site. No. 18 Gramercy Park South was the site of the red brick and brownstone

Luther C. and Julia Clark Mansion, built in 1853 with tall, floor-to-ceiling ground-floor parlor windows, ornate cast-iron balconies and a recessed entrance with a high stoop and two, twelve-foot-high fluted Corinthian columns, along with carved pilasters under a heavy entablature.

Clark was a well-established banker and member of Clark, Dodge & Co. Luther and Julia had six children: George, Arthur, Louis, Ellen, Julia and David. In 1854, Ellen died, and in 1856, Arthur died. Unlike many wealthy New York families who paid to have their sons exempted from the military draft during the Civil War, Luther Clark's twenty-year-old son George C. Clark was picked from the draft lottery in 1864. Luther Clark died in 1877, leaving an estate of $200,000, and was survived by his wife, Julia, and three of his six children. Julia C. Clark, eighty-one years old, died in the mansion in 1900, and it was sold to the Columbia University Club in 1905. The Columbia University Club sold the ex-mansion to the Army and Navy Club in 1918, which, in turn, sold it to a Woman's Club, which was replaced in 1926 by the sixteen-story Parkside Residence Hotel for Women that opened in 1927 with three hundred rooms, all exclusively for women, charging $3.50 a night for a room and full hotel services. It became the Salvation Army's Parkside Evangeline Residence Hall in 1963, still a haven for women only. The basic building still stands, but it was remodeled in 2013 by architect Robert A.M. Stern for Zeckendorf Development into sixteen ultra-luxury condominium residences.

No. 17 Gramercy Park South is now a residency for female students of the School of Visual Arts on East Twenty-third Street, but in the mid-1880s, it was the home of Joseph Pulitzer (1847–1911), who moved to East Fifty-fifth Street and Fifth Avenue in 1887. Pulitzer was the owner/editor of the *New York World* and the *Evening World* newspapers in downtown Manhattan on Newspaper Row. Pulitzer was born in Budapest, Hungry, and as a young man, he was rejected by the Prussian army, the English army and the French Foreign Legion because he couldn't see out of one eye and had poor vision in the other. He came to the United States and in 1864, joined the Union army and served for a year and a half until the end of the Civil War. Pulitzer ended up in St. Louis and worked at small odd jobs until gaining employment at a German American newspaper, where he was able to buy shares. But what actually gave him his start as a publisher was when he married the wealthy Katherine "Kate" Davis (1825–1927) and started his newspaper empire by publishing the *St. Louis Post Dispatch*. Pulitzer left St. Louis in 1883 to escape the public outcry that resulted when one of his editors shot and killed one of his political opponents.

He was passing through Manhattan when he met a financier, Jay Gould, who sold him the *New York World* newspaper. Pulitzer also started publishing the *Evening World* and transformed the *New York World* into one of the nation's most influential papers, bringing in an era of the modern, popular press and a "new journalism" that mixed sensational stunts, entertaining stories and cartoons with serious financial, foreign and political news as well as editorial campaigns that helped change the course of history.

In the late nineteenth century, Pulitzer competed fiercely with William R. Hearst's *Journal* using yellow journalism, a seamy tradition of sex and sensationalism and a style he helped create but abandoned after 1900. It was said that Pulitzer and Hearst's sensationalism helped start the Spanish-American War in 1898. In his later years, Pulitzer supported an anti-expansion policy for the United States in foreign affairs. He also championed the underdog, exposed corrupt insurance companies and crooked politicians and fought injustice. Pulitzer pioneered hiring female reporters, including Nellie Bly (Elizabeth J. Cochrane), who uncovered the corruption on Blackwell's Island Asylum for the newspaper and went on to write *Ten Days in the Mad House* (1887), *Six Months in Mexico* (1888) and *Around the World in Seventy Two Days* (1890).

Pulitzer used his newspapers to expose James Blaine's shady deals to assure Grover Cleveland's presidential victory and led a campaign to erect the pedestal for the Statue of Liberty. Pulitzer defeated Theodore Roosevelt's attempt to have him imprisoned for criminal contempt. One might think he wouldn't have the time, but Pulitzer also had six children by his wife, Kate Davis. In his will, Pulitzer provided the funds to create Grand Army Plaza (Pulitzer Fountain) at the Fifth Avenue entrance to Central Park and to establish the Pulitzer Prizes to be awarded annually in twenty-one categories by Columbia University.

Built as the Valentine B. Hall Gothic Revival mansion in 1845, 16 Gramercy Park South was purchased by Edwin Booth in 1888 for the Players Club (founded in 1887) and was remodeled into a Italian Renaissance clubhouse by Stanford White, who replaced its stoop with an English-style basement entrance and its cast-iron veranda with a distinguished, two-story Tuscan Doric loggia. He also added a handsome roof deck with an iron railing and used elaborately bracketed gas lanterns to flank the main entrance.

The Players Club is a New York City landmark and a national landmark and was an exclusive men's club until May 1989, when it voted to allow women as members. The club retains its original stated purpose to provide a place where "actors and dramatists could mingle in good fellowship with craftsmen of the fine arts, as well as those of the performing arts."

In 1888, Edwin Booth donated his mansion to the Players Club. The third floor was set aside as Booth's personal quarters, and his bedroom is still preserved intact. Booth felt that actors needed to mingle with normal people,

No. 16 Gramercy Park South, the Players Club (formerly the Edwin Booth Mansion).

so its membership has always been mixed, as Booth wanted it. He believed that actors could broaden their minds by socializing with people of diverse educational backgrounds. Charter members included Mark Twain, William T. Sherman and actors John Drew and Lawrence Barrett.

Theater historians consider Edwin Booth America's greatest tragic stage actor. His father was Junius Brutus Booth, a touring Shakespearean star and an eccentric drunk known as the "mad tragedian." Edwin's youngest brother was John Wilkes Booth, the man who assassinated Abraham Lincoln. Edwin Booth was a staunch Unionist and voted for Lincoln; his brother John was a rabid secessionist. After the assassination, Edwin was distraught. He stopped his stage appearances and wrote a letter of public apology. After several months, he returned to the stage. Edwin had three brothers, a sister and a half brother in England, and their sympathies were divided between the North and the South. Three of the brothers—Edwin, Junius Brutus Jr. and John Wilkes—appeared on stage together only once during their long theatrical careers.

They appeared in *Julius Caesar* on November 25, 1864, at the Winter Garden Theater on Mercer Street (between Bleecker Street and West Third Street) in Manhattan. It was a one-time, sold-out performance, and the proceeds went to erect the statue of Shakespeare (1564–1616) by sculptor J.Q.A. Ward on Literary Walk in Central Park. The cornerstone for the

71

Statue of Edwin Booth inside Gramercy Park. *Original watercolor by Ann Woodward.*

statue was laid by Edwin Booth in 1864 to celebrate the 300th anniversary of Shakespeare's birthday, but the dedication wasn't until 1872.

There are any number of melodramatic stories connected to the Booth family. Edwin's father, Junius Brutus Booth, was an established Shakespearean star in England, where he married Adelaide Delannoy in 1815. She was four years older than Junius and toured with him. In 1919, she stopped touring with him when they had a son, Richard. Adelaide wrote to her mother saying, "I am as well as I can be and I am getting as fat as a great beast."

As luck would have it, Junius met the beautiful Mary Ann Holmes (six years younger than he), and she toured with him as his wife had. Well, soon Mary Ann was pregnant, and Junius had a problem. His wife, his father and his son waited for him in London, but Booth loved Mary Ann (and in decades to come, he never looked at another woman). So flight was his answer, and the United States was appealing. (For all his youth, his father asked visitors to bow before a picture of George Washington; being Irish, he had a love of the man who led the American Revolution against England).

Mary Ann and Junius took a forty-four-day voyage on the clipper ship *Two Brothers* to Norfolk, Virginia. They landed in June 1821, and he wrote Adelaide that he had run into trouble with the British stage people, so he would play in America for a time and that he would faithfully send her letters and money—which he did for eighteen years.

In America, Mary Ann Holmes was known as Mrs. Booth. About eighteen years later, his son Richard, in his mid-twenties came to the United States to visit his father in Maryland. He first found that his father was a wild drinker and then that Junius was believed to be married to Mary Ann and they had a family with six children. Richard returned to England and told Adelaide, who promptly boarded a ship sailing to the United States that subsequently was attacked by pirates. Adelaide was abandoned on a Caribbean island. She survived and arrived in America on another ship in October 1846. She confronted Junius publicly by parading with signs in front of Marsh Market in Maryland, expressing her opinion of Junius Booth and calling his family "bastards." Adelaide Delannoy Booth was granted a divorce in April 1851. Junius and Mary Ann were married in May 1851.

The Tilden Mansion was at 15 Gramercy Park South. By 1881, Samuel Tilden (1814–1886) had purchased 14 and 15 Gramercy Park South and had the two houses remodeled into one Victorian Gothic–style forty-room residence by Calvert Vaux (who also designed the Jefferson Market Courthouse and Central Park). Some refer to the style as Gothic Revival in the manner of John Ruskin, with polychromatic brownstone and polished black granite trim. The façade has unusual carvings, with leaf patterns and an occasional "T" for Tilden. It also has a panel that represented literature and the ground-floor library as the theme of the mansion with the five carved heads of William Shakespeare, John Milton, Johann Wolfgang von Goethe, Dante Alighieri and, in the center, Benjamin Franklin by fine arts sculptor Samuel Kitson (1848–1906). In a pediment over one entrance is a bust of Michelangelo executed in 2007 by Sergio R. Morosini (born 1953). The entrance on the left was for residents, and the entrance on the right was for political or literary visitors. Tilden had Donald McDonald convert the three front rooms—with a domed stained-glass ceiling, grand sliding doors and stained-glass windows (designed by John La Farge)—into his library. After Tilden died, the collection became one of the three founding collections (Astor Trust, Lenox Trust and the Tilden Trust) for the New York Public Research Library on Fifth Avenue between West Forty-second Street and West Fortieth Street. The Tilden mansion is both a New York City and a national landmark.

Samuel Tilden passed away in 1886, and by 1890, the mansion became an upscale boardinghouse (the Tilden), which was purchased by the National Arts Club in 1906. The ex-mansion's interior was altered by the club's president, George B. Post, to accommodate the needs of the club.

Samuel Tilden in 1874. *Courtesy of the Library of Congress.*

Post, who was a well-known architect himself, undertook the immediate construction of the National Arts Club Studio Building annex (119 West Nineteenth Street) on the lot that was Tilden's garden in the rear of the club and extended to East Nineteenth Street (see chapter 4). The work inside the ex-mansion revealed a stairway, passageways and a tunnel under the eastern part of the mansion that led to East Nineteenth Street, which many construed to be an escape route built into the mansion in case of assassination attempts.

Assassination? Who was Tilden supposed to be afraid of? Well, the logic was that he was concerned that the Tweed Ring (associates of William M. Tweed) might engineer an attempt on his life. Actually, in the early part of his political career, Tilden enjoyed a friendly working relationship with William Marcy Tweed, but in the post–Civil War era, Tilden became chairman of the Democratic State Committee and began a reform movement in the Democratic Party that led to the demise of William Marcy Tweed. Tilden and the Tweed Ring became political enemies. In 1872, as a member of the New York State Assembly, Tilden played a leading role in the impeachment of Judge George G. Barnard by obtaining legal proof of corruption. These were said to be the reasons for Tilden's escape route. But in answer to these allegations, a close friend of Tilden had a letter sent to the *New York Times* that claimed the passageways were part of an extended wine cellar and a vault was connected to the cellar to accommodate a yearly supply of fuel. Another tunnel, four feet in diameter, was built under the easterly wall of the mansion to provide fresh air for its furnace.

Samuel Tilden was elected governor of New York in 1875 and stepped down in 1876 to run for president of the United States on the Democratic

National Arts Club. *Original watercolor and pen and ink by Ann Woodward.*

ticket against Rutherford Hayes (1822–1893). Tilden won the popular vote, with over 250,000 more votes than Hayes but lost 184 to 185 in the electoral college. Rutherford Hayes became president of the United States after a Congressional commission (eight Republicans and seven Democrats) awarded him twenty contested electoral votes. At what was considered his concession speech at the Manhattan Club, Tilden didn't mince words. To paraphrase part of his speech, Tilden acknowledged that there was no doubt that he was elected president and it had been denied him by the Electoral College and the appointed government commission. He went on to say that he wouldn't claim any personal grievance but the great wrong was to the 4.75 million voters who voted for him and were deprived of their franchise by the nullification of their votes, and the ultimate consequences extended beyond the immediate losers.

A little more information about the National Arts Club, which was founded in 1898 by the literary critic for the *New York Times*, Charles DeKay, as a meeting place for artists, writers and persons active in America's artistic community: It was the first arts club in America to include women from the time it was founded. Theodore Roosevelt was an active member and only one of its many famous members, who included Mark Twain, Robert Henri, Anna Hyatt Huntington, Augustus Saint-Gaudens, Daniel Chester French, William Merritt Chase and Paul Manship.

Robert Henri, seen here in this 1900 photograph at Gramercy Park South. *Courtesy of the Library of Congress.*

Robert Henri (1865–1929) lived, worked and taught at 10 Gramercy Park South from 1909 to 1929. His studio, still intact, has a great northern light. Henri was an extraordinary and charismatic teacher and painter who helped transform American art. He was trained at the Academy of Fine Arts in Philadelphia and in Europe. After returning from Paris, France, he taught art and painting in Philadelphia. John Sloan, George Luks, William Glackens, George Bellows, Rockwell Kent, Edward Hopper and Everett Shinn all were Henri's students in Manhattan, where he taught at the New York School of Art from 1902 to 1908. Henri was elected to the National Academy of Design, and although his paintings hung in important collections across America, the bulk of his income came from teaching.

Robert Henri was a member of a group of painters known as "The Eight" and a progenitor of the Ashcan School. He rejected the genteel styles of painting, such as impressionism, and advocated the unconventional realistic styles depicting robust working-class life. One of his best-known works is *Laughing Child* (Whitney Museum of American Art), and Henri's lecture notes and talks were published as *The Art Spirit* in 1930. It was in the 1890s when Henri encouraged his student John Sloan to paint in a realistic style, and it was Sloan who, in 1908, helped organize the art exhibit at Macbeth Galleries in Manhattan that presented the works of eight independent realistic painters. The show was severely criticized, with one critic suggesting that all their paintings belonged in an ashcan, so the eight artists adopted the name and called themselves the Ashcan Painters. Over time, their works became famous and successful, and the group of painters became known as the Ashcan School of Art.

Chapter 8

MAYOR HARPER TO RUSSELL SAGE

Gramercy Park West to Lexington Avenue

I f we cross over from Gramercy Park South to the Gramercy Park West entrance gate to the park, there is a concrete plaque in the sidewalk. It is located between Gramercy Park South (East Twentieth Street) and Gramercy Park North (East Twenty-first Street), and it commemorates Samuel Ruggles as the founder of Gramercy Park.

Gramercy Park is a tribute to the foresight of Samuel B. Ruggles (1800–1881) and is an excellent example of urban planning. When Ruggles (see chapter 2) developed this area in 1831, he took fifty-two plots (one and a half acres) and deeded them to the sixty surrounding lot owners, establishing the only surviving private park in Manhattan. Ruggles may have been inspired by his frequent visits to St. John's Park (owned by Trinity Church), which was modeled after an eighteenth-century London residential square. So it is fair to say that when Ruggles developed "Manhattan's Four Squares" (Gramercy Square, Stuyvesant Square, Union Square and Madison Square), he was influenced by the design of the eighteenth-century London residential squares—parks surrounded by mansions. Many feel that Gramercy Square survives the best as a wealthy residential neighborhood because its park is private and the other parks are public (their park areas were deeded to the city in an agreement that the city create and maintain the park). Originally, Gramercy Park was restricted to adjacent property owners, but now it is accessible to all who live close by and pay an annual fee. In 1912, there were 383 keys manufactured for park users; of these, 126 are building keys managed by doormen or concierges and signed out by residents. The other

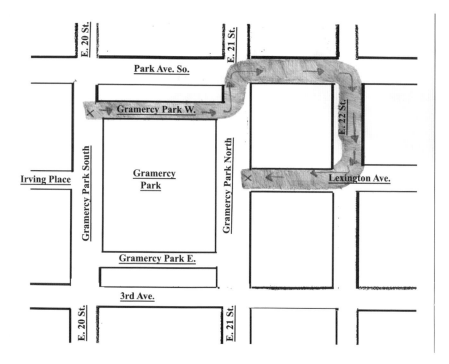

Map of Gramercy Park North, Park Avenue South, East Twenty-second Street and Lexington Avenue.

257 are so-called personal keys. For $350 a year, a condo or co-op owner can buy his or her very own key. If a key is lost, the replacement charge is $1,000.

Some of the original bluestones and some newly cut bluestones were used to re-create the original perimeter sidewalk here. There were a number of cobra head lampposts in the historic district that were thought to be ugly, so many have been replaced with bishop's crook lampposts.

If we look across the street from the Gramercy Park West entrance we see 4 Gramercy Park West, a red brick Greek Revival house. Designed by Alexander Jackson Davis (1803–1892), it was built in 1844 with cast-iron and lacework-decorated verandas that would fit in nicely on the balconies of a house in the French Quarter of New Orleans. The mayor's lamps at the entrance were installed in 1848 when ex-mayor James Harper (1795–1869) purchased the house. He lived here until he died in a carriage accident in 1869. Harper was elected mayor on the American Republican (anti-immigration and anti-Catholicism) party ticket and served as mayor from 1844 to 1845 (a one-year term). He replaced the old night watch system with the city's first municipal police force. Harper was able to select only two hundred men for the force before he was out of office, but successor William Havemeyer expanded the force to eight hundred and established local station houses. Harper also banished free-roaming pigs and cattle from the city streets and started to establish a citywide sanitation system. He was subsequently put forward for the governorship of the state, but he preferred to run Harper & Brothers Publishing, the business firm he and his brothers founded.

Harper had started work as a printer's apprentice at the age of fifteen. In 1817, at twenty-two years old, Harper and his brother John started a printing business with $500 they had saved, plus a loan from their father. They mostly did work for other businesses, and by 1830, the business had grown and there were the four brothers (James, John, Wesley and Fletcher) as partners. Their printing process progressed from hand power to horse

JAMES HARPER ESQ.

Mayor of the City of New York

James Harper in 1844, a founder of Harper and Brothers Publishing and mayor of New York City from 1844 to 1845. *Courtesy of the Library of Congress.*

power. A young horse in the cellar of the house next door to the factory was harnessed to a beam attached to a shaft that operated the press, and the horse would walk round and round, providing power to move the press—with no lunch break.

In 1962, Harper & Brothers became Harper & Row when it merged with Row, Peterson & Co. In 1987, Harper & Row was acquired by the News Corporation, and in 1990, the company merged with William Collins publishers and became HarperCollins, which had sales in the United States of $1.162 million in 2004 and employed over three thousand people worldwide.

Next door, 3 Gramercy Park West was built as a mirror image of 4 Gramercy Park West. Both were designed by Alexander Jackson Davis in 1844. Iris Whitney, an actress and interior decorator, was living at 3 Gramercy Park West in 1952 when actor John Garfield (1913–1952) died here in bed of a heart attack. Rumors were that he died in the bed of Iris Whitney, but in the 1975 biography by Larry Swindell, *Body & Soul: The Story of John Garfield*, it is stated that Garfield was in a guest room accompanied only by a glass of orange juice when he had the heart attack. Garfield was blacklisted because he had refused to give names of friends and associates he knew to be Communists to the House Un-American Activities Committee (HUAC) hearings in 1951. Even though he had never been a member of the Communist party, he did have leftist views and sympathies. His best remembered films include *The Postman Always Rings Twice* (1946), *Humoresque* (1946), *Body and Soul* (1947) and *Force of Evil* (1948), and he had a supporting role in *Gentleman's Agreement* (1947). In all his roles, he brought his characterizations to life with great passion and skill.

At the turn of the last century, 2 Gramercy Park West was home to Gifford Pinchot (1845–1946), who served from 1905 to 1910 as the first chief of the U.S. Forest Service (America's first professional forester). On April 6, 1896, Pinchot used his home here to host the wedding reception of Mary Scott Dimmick and Benjamin Harrison (1833–1901), the former twenty-sixth president of the United States (1889–93). Pinchot later was twice elected governor of Pennsylvania in 1922 and in 1931. Pinchot reformed the management and development of forests in the United States and was the first to demonstrate the practicality and profitability of managing forests for continuous cropping. He advocated scientific forestry and the controlled, profitable use of the natural resources to benefit mankind—"the art of producing from the forest whatever it can yield for the service of man."

No. 1 Gramercy Park West, an Italianate-style brownstone mansion, was home to Dr. Valentine Mott (1785–1865), who moved here in 1849 with his

Gifford Pinchot, first chief of the U.S. Forest Service and twice governor of Pennsylvania. *Courtesy of the Library of Congress.*

wife, Louisa, and their nine children. Mott was one of the most renowned surgeons in the days before the Civil War. He was responsible for founding NYU Medical College and Bellevue Hospital, and from 1809 to 1826, he held a Chair of Surgery at Columbia College and resigned to found Rutgers Medical Center (disbanded). Dr. Mott was also president of the New York Academy of Medicine and strongly favored using cadavers in surgical instruction, an idea that was considered sacrilegious at that time.

Facing Gramercy Park West is a co-op apartment building, 60 Gramercy Park North, built in 1928 and designed by Emery Roth with sixteen floors and 121 apartments. The building goes through to East Twenty-second Street and has fanciful pinnacles at the tenth- and sixteenth-floor set backs

Above: No. 1 Gramercy Park West, the home of Dr. Valentine Mott.

Left: Dr. Valentine Mott lived at 1 Gramercy Park West from 1849 to 1865. *Courtesy of the Library of Congress.*

and rises to a pinnacle at the penthouse level that sports a red tile gable roof, a water tower decorated with eagles and elongated triple arches executed in a harmonious mode. The façade is embellished with a modest mix of Italian and Spanish Renaissance motifs, ornamental terra-cotta window surrounds and cast-iron loggias.

Before 1927, on the site of 60 Gramercy Park North, there were three mid-nineteenth-century Gramercy Park mansions facing Gramercy Park West: the George Templeton Strong mansion at 55 Gramercy Park North, the Olivia Templeton mansion at 57 Gramercy Park North and the Philip Kearny mansion at 59 Gramercy Park North. Each one was four stories tall and three bays wide. Historically, the most important resident of these mansions was George Templeton Strong (1820–1875) because he chronicled in detail the nineteenth-century life of Manhattan residents. Especially interesting are his recordings of the thoughts, hopes and fears of New Yorkers in the periods before and after the Civil War. The original text of his 2,250-page diary is housed at the New York Historical Society at 170 Central Park West. You can find hardcover and paperback copies at the New York City Public Library. Strong's diary is a brilliant guide to a journey back through time.

As a young man, Strong distinguished himself practicing law in his father's office. George T. Strong married Ellen Ruggles (Samuel Ruggles's daughter) in 1848, and several months later, they moved to 55 Gramercy Park North. The lot was a wedding gift from his father-in-law, Samuel Ruggles, and his father built the house.

Ellen Ruggles Strong was a gentle, devoted, lively companion and a tireless worker for the Union cause. During the Civil War era, they both traveled extensively raising funds for the cause, and George and Ellen also sponsored fairs.

We will now walk west on Gramercy Park North (East Twenty-first Street) to 61 Gramercy Park North, Calvary Church, completed in 1848 on the northeast corner of Park Avenue South. It is part of the Gramercy Park Historic District and was designed by James Renwick Jr. (who also designed Grace Church at Broadway and East Ninth Street and, later, St. Patrick's Cathedral on Fifth Avenue between East Fiftieth Street and East Fifty-first Street) in the Gothic Revival style (a mix of traditional English and European ideas), with twin wooden spires that deteriorated and were removed in the 1860s. The interior has a five-sided apse, a free-standing altar that you can walk around (not one against the east wall), and forty-two clerestory windows with a tin skylight for each one. George T. Strong described its ceiling as a "paradise of tinsmithry" in his diary.

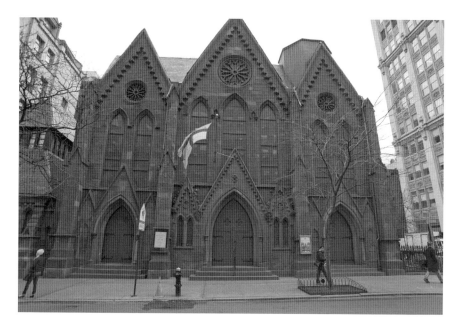

Calvary Church, located at 277 Park Avenue South at the northeast corner of East Twenty-first Street.

This Episcopal congregation was formed in 1835, and Eleanor Roosevelt was baptized in this church in 1885. Inside windows commemorate the memory of Rowland Hazard II. In 1931, Hazard realized he was an alcoholic and became a patient of Carl Jung in Zurich, Germany, when unexpectedly, Jung told him that further treatment would be of no use and that Hazard needed to be caught up in a religious experience. Rowland returned and found spiritual experience through a group at Calvary Church. Under the rectorship of Samuel Shoemaker (1893–1963), the Calvary Church Mission had extensive outreach activities, including evangelical programs for office workers and programs for alcoholics. It was here in 1934, at a program called Moral Rearmament, that Hazard met Bob Wilson (1895–1971), an alcoholic who collaborated with Dr. Robert Smith of Akron, Ohio, in the self-help methods of the Oxford Group, emphasizing personal transformation, self control and faith in God. In 1939, Wilson published *Alcoholics Anonymous*, a lasting best seller, and in 1953, his second book, *Twelve Steps and Twelve Traditions*, was published and is now a model for many other self-help programs.

In the mid-1970s, Calvary Church formed a united parish with the Church of the Holy Communion (at Sixth Avenue and West Twenty-first Street) and

CALVARY CHURCH,

Erected 1846-7.

New York published by Samuel A. Deare, Sexton.

Calvary Church was erected 1846 to 1847 and is seen here with its spires. *Courtesy of the Library of Congress.*

A Gothic Revival pavilion on the north side of Calvary Church.

with St. George's Episcopal Church at Stuyvesant Square (a congregation that had been active since the Revolutionary War). They combined parishes and alternate using churches to save on expenses.

The little Gothic Revival pavilion next to the north side of Calvary Church was designed in 1867 by James Renwick Jr. as the Sunday School Building. It is now rented as office space.

Directly across at the northwest corner of East Twenty-first Street, we see 270 Park Avenue South. There was a luxury apartment building on this site where David O. Selznick (1902–1965) lived as a teenager from 1916 to the early 1920s with his father, Lewis, a successful silent movie producer; his mother; and his elder brother, Myron. They all lived in a luxurious twenty-two-room apartment with servants and a chauffeured Rolls Royce. David attended Columbia University. But in 1923, Lewis J. Selznick went bankrupt, and in 1926, David left for California without funds, but with his father's connections, he was able to get a job as an assistant story editor at Metro-Goldwyn-Mayer. David moved from studio to studio, working his way up to director and producer, and created his own studio by the time he was thirty-three years of age. His best-remembered contributions include producing the film *Gone With the Wind* and bringing English director Alfred Hitchcock to Hollywood in 1939.

Now walk one short block north to 281 Park Avenue South, a New York City landmark and a national landmark, built by Calvary Church and opened in 1894 at the southeast corner of East Twenty-second Street as the Church Mission House. It was restored in 1991 and renamed the Protestant Welfare Agencies Headquarters building, the primary function of which was to rent space to nonprofit organizations. The building was sold in 2015 for $50 million. The restoration architects are Kapell & Kostow of Manhattan. The original architects, R.W. Gibson & Edward J.N. Stent, designed the steel-frame building with an eclectic façade that has been described as Northern European Gothic, as flamboyant Romanesque Revival and even as Dutch Renaissance. Robert W. Gibson was one of the first New York architects to work in this mode, using medieval arcading, sculptural Gothic clustered shafts and moldings to organize the façade into a rectangular framework concealing the steel frame's grid and changing the grid's regularity into a positive virtue. Gibson also used corner tourelles, a sculptured tympanum, roof dormers and patterns of low relief terra-cotta decorations in his eclectic design. The design of this building is an early example of using the Gothic style on the façade of a skyscraper. Later, Gothic "piers" and decorations embellished the façades on skyscrapers such as the U.S. Realty Building, which opened in 1907; the Trinity Building, opened in 1908; and the Woolworth Building, which opened in 1913.

If we look from the northeast corner of East Twenty-second Street and Park Avenue South toward Lexington Avenue, we will see some of the buildings that are part of a proposed extension to the Gramercy Park Historic District. The United Charities Building at 285 Park Avenue South, also known as 105 East Twenty-second Street, opened in 1893 and was designed by the prolific architect Robert H. Robertson and Rowe and Baker with a Classical façade. A bit unusual is the fact that the building is listed on the National Register of Historic Places but not designated as a New York City landmark. Possibly the explanation can be found in the fourth edition of the *AIA Guide to New York City*'s description of the building as "not one of Robertson's better buildings—boring even with its decorations." But the building has national significance because it housed the Charity Organization Society, which represented the combined resources of many Protestant charities, including members of over one thousand prominent families and more than five hundred churches and societies across the United States.

The United Charities Building was constructed by John S. Kennedy, a wealthy banker, for the New York Association for Improving the Conditions of the Poor. The building is now owned by the Community Service Society

No. 281 Park Avenue South, the Protestant Welfare Agency Headquarters Building, formerly the Church Mission House.

for the purpose of improving the conditions of the working class and to elevate their physical state. The building also houses the Children's Aid Society and other charitable institutions.

This building was used as a base by some of the Progressive Era's most influential women's groups to plan a number of reform-oriented goals, with associations like the Charity Organization Society, the National Consumers League and the National Child Labor Committee. These were among the first reformist organizations that had a strong voice in creating government policies. This building harbored leaders like Florence Kelley and researchers like Josephine Goldmark—women who helped mold our country's modern role in social issues. It was a group of organizations in this building that helped convince Theodore Roosevelt to create the federally funded U.S. Children's Bureau, a group essential in ending child labor in America. These were some of the Progressive Era's most influential women's groups that lobbied for labor laws to foster better labor conditions and influence future policies.

Back on the south side of the street at 102 East Twenty-second Street, opened in 1928, is the Gramercy Arms, a ten-story, Art Deco apartment house with polychromatic glazed terra-cotta panels under the second, fifth, seventh and ninth floors. Sugarman & Berger, the firm that designed this apartment

A gargoyle on the Collegiate Gothic façade of 127 East Twenty-second Street, formerly the Manhattan Trade School for Girls.

house, had previously specialized in designing Renaissance-decorated middle-income apartment houses, and this was its first Art Deco design.

As we walk east to Lexington Avenue, we cannot help but notice the building on the northwest corner of East Twenty-second Street and Lexington Avenue that was the Manhattan Trade School for Girls, which opened in 1919 at 127 East Twenty-second Street. Later known as the Mabel Dean Bacon Vocational High School, it is now the New Manhattan High School Collaborative and the School of the Future (NYC), which accepts students citywide through applications and interviews for the sixth to the twelfth grades. It was founded by Apple Inc. in 1990.

The original architect, C.B.J. Snyder, designed a girls' vocational school building shaped like a commercial loft building in the Garment District (where many of the girls would find employment), but he embellished it with Collegiate Gothic–styled decorations that include fanciful gargoyles, some with books and tools, at the cornice level. This is a metal-frame building enclosed by a façade that is limestone on the ground floor and all terra cotta above.

Across the avenue on the southeast corner of East Twenty-second Street is a generic apartment house that opened in 1951 at 7 Lexington Avenue. On its façade is a plaque commemorating Peter Cooper (1791–1883), who lived in

Peter Cooper. *Original pen and ink drawing by Ann Woodward.*

his mansion on the site from 1851 until he died in 1883. The mansion then went to his brother-in-law, Abram Hewitt (1822–1903), who was mayor of New York from 1886 to 1887. Hewitt's daughters, Amy, Eleanor and Sara, stored a huge decorative arts collection in the mansion that became the core collection for the Cooper-Hewitt National Design Museum, housed in the old Carnegie mansion on Fifth Avenue.

Peter Cooper was a manufacturer, inventor, philanthropist, entrepreneur and real estate investor. He started with a glue factory, using abandoned horse carcasses that he got from the streets of Manhattan. Cooper founded an iron foundry, built America's first steam locomotive (Thom Thumb) and invented Jell-o. Cooper ran unsuccessfully for president of the United States in 1876 on the Greenback ticket and lost to Rutherford Hayes. He also founded Cooper Union College for the Advancement of Science and Art as a private college that did not charge tuition until 2013. It was the first college in the United States to offer free higher education to the daughters and sons of working-class people and the first to have a library reading room open to the public. At the dedication of Cooper Union, Peter Cooper said he thought that "too many good women were tied to no-good men simply because they lacked the means to make a living."

Look across Lexington Avenue at the southwest corner of East Twenty-second Street to see 4 Lexington Avenue. Opened in 1915 as the Russell Sage Foundation Building, it was converted to Sage House (apartments) in 1975. The building is a New York City landmark and has an ornate façade that describes the purposes of the building. It is crowned with a deep cornice embellished with small grotesque and cherubic gargoyles and is designed after a Renaissance palazzo adapted to the needs of an office building. The building has a tripartite horizontal street-level massing and a rhythmic arrangement of round arch openings reminiscent of a Florentine palazzo. The Kingstone and rockface brownstone façade has panels in the form of shields expressing the ideals and goals of the foundation: Work, Play, Housing, Religion, Education, Civics and Justice. Rectangular panels on the Twenty-second Street façade represent the specialized work of the foundation: Study, Service and Counsel, and a frieze is inscribed with "For the Improvement of Social and Living Conditions." The use of decoration to symbolically communicate the purpose of the building was common with architects trained in the Beaux Arts practices like Grosvenor Atterbury. Many of the city's late nineteenth- and early twentieth-century public and institutional buildings are enhanced in such a way.

The foundation was initially endowed by Margaret O. Sage (1828–1918) with $10 million with the goal of promoting the improvement of social and living conditions for the poor. The foundation has been active in developing social work and urban planning as professions and has supported progressive activities. Margaret Sage is remembered for sponsoring Forest Hills Gardens in Queens and Russell Sage College as a women's college in Troy, New York,

among dozens of other causes she supported. She inherited between $50 million and $70 million when her husband, Russell Sage, who was a financier, a railroad executive and a politician, died in 1906. Margaret Sage spent the last twelve years of her life giving his fortune away. She started by creating the Russell Sage Foundation in 1907 and continued giving until she gave away over $80 million by the time she died in 1918.

There is some irony here, especially if one knows about her husband, Russell Sage (1816–1906), who was well known as a tight-fisted miser. There were stories that floated around about his stinginess, but one made the newspapers in 1891 when a mentally

Mrs. Russell Sage. *Courtesy of the Library of Congress.*

disturbed man from Connecticut, Henry L. Norcross, came to Sage's second-floor office at 71 Broadway on December 4. With ten pounds of explosives in a bag, Norcross demanded $1.2 million or he said he was going to blow up New York City's meanest man. A clerk in Sage's office, William R. Laidlaw Jr., claimed that Sage then grabbed him and used him as a shield as Norcross dropped the bag and an explosion destroyed the office, killing Norcross, badly wounding the clerk and blowing Benjamin F. Norton out of the window into Trinity cemetery—but leaving Sage unharmed. Sage denied using Laidlaw as a shield, and Laidlaw ended up winning a court judgment of $43,000 against Sage, but Sage fought paying the court judgment with all his lawyers and Laidlaw was never able to collect a penny.

Since we are on Lexington Avenue, it seems appropriate for me to mention that it was not part of Manhattan's original street grid created by the Commissioner's Plan of 1811 (with John Randel Jr. as chief engineer). In 1840, Ruggles persuaded New York State to insert an avenue between Third Avenue and Fourth Avenue (later called Park Avenue South). From Gramercy Park going north, he suggested the avenue be called Lexington after the famous Battle of Lexington ("the shot heard round the world"), and from Gramercy Park to East Fourteenth Street, he named the avenue for his friend Washington Irving.

Chapter 9

ATLANTIC CABLE TO KNIGHTS IN ARMOR

LEXINGTON AVENUE AND
GRAMERCY PARK NORTH

As we walk to 50 Gramercy Park North, also known as 1 Lexington Avenue, we are stepping from the Gramercy Park neighborhood back into the official Gramercy Park Historic District. There is a plaque on the northeast corner of Lexington Avenue and Gramercy Park North commemorating the site of the Cyrus West Field Mansion.

Cyrus West Field (1819–1892) was an industrialist who started young, going from job to job building his skills, and made his fortune in the paper manufacturing business before he was forty years old. He and a group of associates (including Peter Cooper) formed the New York, Newfoundland & London Telegraph Co. and laid the first trans-Atlantic telegraph cable in 1866. He built the Third Avenue elevated train between 1877 and 1879 but lost it a few years later to financier and railroad tycoon Jay Gould. In 1900, Cyrus W. Field's mansion and that of his brother David Dudley Field next door (49 Gramercy Park North) were sold to Henry Poor, who hired Stanford White (who lived across the street) to combine them into a single grand mansion. This new structure lasted only until 1909, when it was replaced by the twelve-story apartment building cooperative at 1 Lexington Avenue.

Henry V. Poor's *History of the Railroads and Canals of the United States* was published in 1860, and it quickly became the most valuable financial source of its day and a precursor to financial and investment publications in the United States. Poor's Publishing Co. and Standard Statistics Co. merged in 1941 into Standard & Poor's, which, in 1966, became a

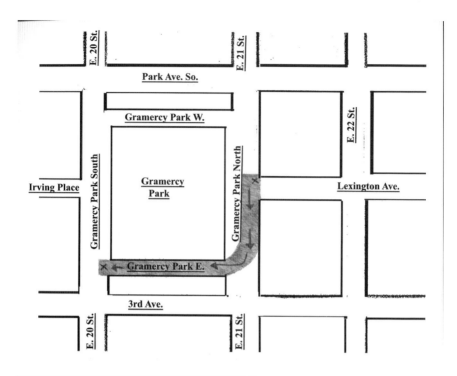

Above: Map of Gramercy Park North and Gramercy Park East.

Left: Cyrus Field. *Courtesy of the Library of Congress.*

subsidiary of McGraw Hill and now has fifty financial publications in print and electronic forms available to business and government agencies. Its office is at 25 Broadway.

Cyrus W. Field had three brothers: Stephen, Henry and David Dudley, who was an associate justice of the U.S. Supreme Court. All the brothers had mansions on Gramercy Park North.

Across the street at 55 Gramercy Park North is the site of Stanford White's mansion on the northwest corner of Lexington Avenue and Gramercy Park North. Stanford White (1853–1906) is remembered as the most prominent architect of the Gilded Age. He and his firm, McKim, Mead & White, were leading proponents of Beaux Arts architecture. With the numerous mansions, institutional and religious buildings they designed throughout New York City, New York State and the United States, they defined the "American Renaissance." Stanford White's father, Richard Grant White, was a Shakespearean scholar with no money but a lot of connections in New York's art world, including John LaFarge, Lewis Comfort Tiffany and Frederick Law Olmstead, among others. Stanford had no formal architectural training but worked for six years as the assistant to Henry Hobson Richardson, the well-known American architect who created the style that is recognized to this day as Richardsonian Romanesque. In 1878, Stanford White, Charles F. McKim and Augustus Saint Gaudens (they were known as the "three redheads") spent eighteen months in Europe taking their own grand tour. Upon returning to New York, Stanford White and Charles F. McKim joined with William R. Mead to found the McKim, Mead & White partnership, and all commissions were signed by McKim, Mead & White, never by an individual architect.

Stanford White was the victim of the infamous "murder of the century" by jealous millionaire Harry Thaw, who shot White in the back of the head three times in front of hundreds of witnesses at the old Madison Square Garden rooftop restaurant in 1906. Ironically, this was a building White had designed and was part owner of, along with Andrew Carnegie and J.P. Morgan.

Thaw, who was mentally disturbed from childhood, was insanely jealous of a past affair between his wife, Evelyn Nesbit (nicknamed "the world's most beautiful woman"), and Stanford White. Because he kept hearing stories of the earlier seduction and Evelyn's confession, he claimed "Dementia Americana," saying he had to vindicate the honor of his wife. Thaw's trials were held at the Jefferson Market Courthouse (now a public library). The first trial ended with a hung jury, but the second trial resulted in Thaw being sent to Matteawan State Hospital for the Criminally Insane for seven years.

Evelyn Nesbit, 1900. *Courtesy of the Library of Congress.*

In 1917, Thaw was convicted for kidnapping, whipping and sexual assault on Francis Gump, a nineteen-year-old boy from Kansas. Thaw was confined for six years in Kirkbride Asylum in Philadelphia. Ironically, White's mansion was sold to the Princeton Club, where, in front of its entrance in 1911, the "literary murder of the century" occurred. (See the section on David G. Phillips in chapter 4).

By 1925, the Gramercy Park Hotel at 53 Gramercy Park North replaced the old mansion, and the hotel still retains several of Stanford White's fireplaces. The hotel's original architect was Robert T. Lyons (1873–1956), and the extension in 1930 was designed by Thompson & Churchill. In 1927, Joseph P. Kennedy and family rented the whole second floor of the hotel for the summer when John F. Kennedy, future president of the United States, was a young boy, and he played in Gramercy Park that summer.

In the 1940s, the literary and social critic Edmund Wilson and wife, novelist Mary McCarthy (1912–1989), were living at the hotel. Humorist, author and screenwriter S.J. Perelman (1904–1979) died here in apartment 1621 at seventy-five years old.

Humphrey Bogart (1899–1957) married the successful stage actress Helen Menken (1901–1966) in the hotel lobby in 1926. She was living in the hotel, and he just moved in. Even though they had been a couple for several years before, the marriage lasted a little over a year, and after the divorce, they remained lifelong friends.

Bogart had started his acting career on the stage in 1921 and was in twenty-one Broadway productions between 1922 and 1935, all in secondary mediocre roles. In 1934, Bogart and Leslie Howard (1893–1943) became friends while acting in *The Petrified Forest*, a smash hit, and they had agreed that neither would do the movie without the other. When Warner Brothers bought the film rights to the play, they wanted Howard for the lead but not Bogart as the villain. Leslie Howard refused to do it without Bogart. Warner Brothers relented, and Bogart was signed to play the villain, Duke Mantee. The film was released in 1936, and the rest is history. Bogart named one of his children Leslie Howard Bogart.

In 2003, the Gramercy Park Hotel was owned and renovated by Ian Schrager in collaboration with artist Julian Schnabel, who designed interiors, fixtures and furniture pieces in the hotel. The hotel was sold in 2010 and is now owned by RFR Holding LLC and operated by Manhattan Hospitality Advisors. The Rose Bar, the Jade Bar and the rooftop Gramercy Terrace restaurant are standing attractions at the hotel, along with Danny Meyer's Maialino restaurant. The hotel exhibits paintings by noted artists, including Jean-Michel Basquiat, Damien Hirst, Richard Prince, Julian Schnabel, Cy Twombly and Andy Warhol.

We are now walking east to 44 Gramercy Park North, an apartment building that opened in 1930 and was designed by Schwartz & Gross with two different heights. The part of the building facing the park is fifteen stories, and the section facing East Twenty-first Street is twenty-one stories.

The building has a striking façade with Neo-Gothic details that include a limestone pointed arch entrance, leaded-glass windows on the ground floor, drip lintels, modest gables, crenelated parapets and terra-cotta balconies pierced by quatrefoils. The three upper floors on both sections have brick diaperwork and windows with their original multipaned metal casements. In all, it is an intricate design worth taking the time to appreciate.

In a building previously on this site, the poet Hart Crane (1899–1932) rented a two-room apartment that he shared with his mother and grandmother in the summer of 1917. He was eighteen years old and getting his first poem published. In 1924, Crane began *The Bridge*, his epic poem that was partly inspired by the Brooklyn Bridge and celebrated the American experience in terms of a higher intelligence. By this time, he seemed to be psychologically disturbed and an alcoholic. In 1932, he traveled to Mexico on a Guggenheim fellowship, and on his return trip, he committed suicide by jumping off the boat in the Gulf of Mexico, into the sea that he often uses to symbolize love and/or death in his poems. Crane was an American poet in the tradition of Blake and Emerson because he tried to answer the despair of the 1920s, and contemporary poets are still influenced by his work. He was born in Ohio and spent his youth in Cleveland, where his father was a successful candy manufacturer.

A few doors down, going toward Third Avenue, we see 39½ Gramercy Park North. A building that used to occupy this site was home to Norman Thomas (1884–1968) during the final years of his life from 1949 to 1968 (see the last paragraph of chapter 3).

Across the street is 38 Gramercy Park North, which was home to John Steinbeck (1902–1968) in 1925. He rented a small room here for seven dollars a week and wrote short stories while working as a cub reporter for the *New York World*. He got fired, and then he decided to stay in his room and write night and day. For the most part, he ate sardines from a can and crackers and felt dejected because he couldn't get his stories published, so he ended up returning to California in late 1926.

Once back in California, Steinbeck developed into a successful writer, producing twenty-seven books that included sixteen novels, six nonfiction books and five collections of short stories. Some of his best works include *Of Mice and Men, East of Eden, Cannery Row, To a God Unknown, Travels with Charley in Search of America* and *Grapes of Wrath*, for which he won the Pulitzer Prize in 1940.

For many years early in his life, Steinbeck worked at hard physical jobs, and it seems this had a profound effect on his writing and his personality. He is sometimes described as private, straightforward and even as a shy person. But actually, his books reveal him as an intelligent, complex man with a strong idea of how America should be—a country with opportunity for all, without prejudice or poverty. Steinbeck won the Nobel Prize for Literature in 1962. He married three times, to Carol Henning, Gwyndolyn Conger and Elaine Anderson Scott, and had two sons, Thom and John.

And now we walk back to 36 Gramercy Park East, a twelve-story, cooperative apartment building that opened in 1910, turned rental in 1946 and returned to a cooperative in 2009. It was built by John E. Olson and designed by James Riley Gordon (1863–1937) with an all terra-cotta, Gothic Revival façade painted white. Gordon was a prominent Texas-trained architect who won the Congressional medal for the Texas State Building in the 1893 Chicago World's Fair. At 36 Gramercy Park East, he demonstrates his judgment using Gothic details that serve the dual purpose of accenting a tall metal frame building and blending in with Gramercy Park's older Gothic-styled mansions that were still here at the time. His eye-catching Gothic details include arches, colonnettes, shields, cherubs and six outstanding grotesque gargoyles, along with intricate tracery, rope molding and two silver-painted, cast-stone knights in armor and holding spears that guard the entrance. We also must mention its projecting oriels (from the

The façade of 36 Gramercy Park East.

fourth to tenth floors). The basement is clad with dressed ashlar granite and has square headed windows with metal grates. There is a deeply recessed central entrance on the U-shaped building, creating an illusion of two identical towers.

Besides Gothic Revival, the building's style is sometimes referred to as French Gothic or even Francis I French Renaissance (because of its plaques with a shield and a crown in the spandrels). Whatever you call it, the building does attract your attention.

Famous residents included circus magnate Alfred Ringling, writer Eugene O'Neill, sculptor Daniel Chester French (Lincoln Memorial) and actor John Barrymore, who was the first actor to break fellow Gramercy Park resident Edwin Booth's record of one hundred consecutive performances of *Hamlet* on Broadway.

We are now going to leave the Gramercy Park Historic District and walk through what is considered part of the Gramercy Park neighborhood and will join us with the Union Square Historic District and neighborhood.

Chapter 10

THEODORE ROOSEVELT TO TAMMANY HALL

East Twentieth Street to Seventeenth Street

Now we will walk west on Gramercy Park North to see 250 Park Avenue South, at the southwest corner of East Twentieth Street, a twelve-story industrial building, designed by Rouse and Goldstone in 1911, with a terra-cotta, Neo-Gothic façade that includes great, grotesque, winged monster gargoyles boldly protruding twelve stories high at the top of the building and also at the corner and elsewhere on the façade.

Directly across the avenue at the southeast corner of East Twentieth Street at the site of 245 Park Avenue South (Fourth Avenue in 1855), there once stood All Souls Unitarian Church, Manhattan's (and America's) first Byzantine-style church. It was designed by Jacob Wrey Mould (1825–1886), an architect best remembered for his contributions to the design of Central Park and for bringing High Victorian architecture to the United States. Famous New Yorkers who worshiped here included industrialist and philanthropist Peter Cooper; orator and editor/owner of the *New York Post*, William Cullen Bryant; and author Herman Melville. The church was demolished in the early 1930s, and the congregation moved to 1157 Lexington Avenue at East Eightieth Street.

Now walk west on East Twentieth Street to 28 East Twentieth Street, the Theodore Roosevelt Birthplace National Historic Site. Theodore Roosevelt (1858–1919) was the twenty-sixth president of the United States (from 1901 to 1909) and is the only president who was born and raised in New York City. His three-story brownstone home stood on this site. It was built in 1848 and purchased by the Roosevelt family in 1854. Teddy lived here with his

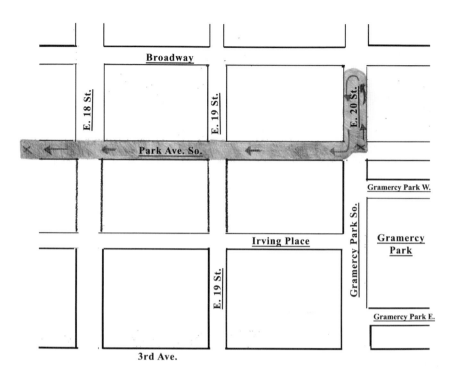

Map of East Twentieth Street from Park Avenue South to East Seventeenth Street.

The grotesque gargoyles on the façade at 250 Park Avenue South.

All Souls Unitarian Church. *Original pen and ink drawing by Ann Woodward.*

family until 1872, when they moved to West Fifty-seventh Street when he was fourteen years old.

Theodore Roosevelt was born into a wealthy Manhattan family, but he was a sickly child and suffered from asthma. Teddy exercised and engaged in a strenuous life, increasing his physical strength. He was home-schooled and attended Harvard College, where he studied biology, boxed and developed an interest in naval affairs. By 1881, Teddy was elected to the New York State Assembly and became a leader of the Republican Party's reform faction. In 1882, he wrote *The Naval War of 1812*. Roosevelt was a politician, author, naturalist, soldier, explorer and historian, and he was also the first president to win the Nobel Peace Prize in 1906 for negotiating the end of the Russo-Japanese War. He was appointed police commissioner of New York City in 1895 and assistant secretary to the navy in 1897. He was elected governor of New York in 1899 and then served as vice president of the United States, becoming president when President William McKinley was assassinated in 1901. Theodore Roosevelt was elected president of the United States in 1904, and his image enhances Mount Rushmore, along with those of George Washington, Thomas Jefferson and Abraham Lincoln.

No. 28 East Twentieth Street, the Theodore Roosevelt Museum.

The room where Theodore Roosevelt was born at 28 East Twentieth Street. *Courtesy of the Library of Congress.*

The Roosevelt townhouse was demolished in 1916, and in 1919, the site was purchased by the Women's Roosevelt Memorial Association. Theodate Pope Riddle was commissioned to rebuild a replica of the Roosevelt home and to design the museum next door. At the time, the surviving house next door (which used to be Teddy's uncle's home at 26 East Twentieth Street) was a twin to the Roosevelt home and was used as a model. After Theodore Roosevelt's home was recreated, Riddle replaced 26 East Twentieth Street with the museum. The new house was rededicated in 1923 and refurbished with furnishings from the original Roosevelt home. Teddy's widow and his sisters provided information about and furnishings for the interior. In 1953, the Women's Roosevelt Memorial Association merged with the Roosevelt Memorial Association.

Theodate Pope Riddle (1867–1946) is considered the first successful female architect in America. She designed schools, private homes and estates in Connecticut and New York, her masterpiece being the unusual medieval school and campus of Avon Old Farms School in Connecticut. Riddle practiced architecture for over thirty years, working at times with McKim, Mead & White. She was a survivor on the *Lusitania* in 1915, and she was elected to the American Institute of Architects (AIA) and inducted into the Connecticut Women's Hall of Fame.

From 28 East Twentieth Street, we will walk east to Park Avenue South, then south to East Eighteenth Street and take a right turn to the Old Town Bar at 45 East Eighteenth Street, which opened in the 1890s as a German saloon called Viemeister's. During Prohibition, it operated as Craig's Restaurant, a speakeasy with Tammany's protection. After 1933, it became known as the Old Town Bar, and its neon sign was installed in 1937. Much of today's interior is original, including the fifty-five-foot-long mahogany and marble bar (originally a lunch counter), its sixteen-foot-high tin ceilings and its large beveled-edge plate mirror. The men's bathroom has huge urinals that date back to 1910. Upstairs used to be the "Ladies and Gentlemen's Dining Room," and its dumbwaiters are New York's oldest restaurant conveyors that are still in use.

We are now walking south one block on Park Avenue South to 50 Union Square, also known as 201 Park Avenue South, a New York City landmark office building that opened in 1911 on the northeast corner of Park Avenue South and East Seventeenth Street as the Germania Life Insurance Co. Building. It changed its name during World War I to the Guardian Life Insurance Co. Building because of anti-German emotions running high at the time. It has a twenty-story, Renaissance Revival–influenced façade

Above: No. 50 Union Square, the W New York Union Square Hotel, formerly the Guardian Life Insurance Co. Building.

Left: Theodore Dreiser. *Courtesy of the Library of Congress.*

designed by Alfred D'Oench (D'Oench & Yost) with an impressive copper, four-story French Mansard roof that crowns the building with its reddish-orange terra-cotta tiles and various-shaped dormers—all topped with a large electric sign displaying the company's name. There are small grotesque gargoyles between the first and second floors. The insurance company occupied the first four floors and rented the rest for office space.

In January 1925, the novelist Theodore Dreiser (1871–1945) rented a small office in this building for peace and quiet to finish his novel *An American Tragedy*. Dreiser had earlier novels and short stories published, but *American Tragedy* was his first real commercial success, and he was to become rich after many years of struggling. Dreiser was living in Brooklyn at the time with his companion and cousin, Helen Richardson, whom he eventually married in 1944. Dreiser was involved in several campaigns against social injustice, including the union leader Tom Mooney's conviction in 1916; the lynching of Frank Little, an Industrial Workers of the World (IWW) leader, in 1917; Emma Goldman's deportation in 1919; and the Sacco and Vanzetti case in 1927. From 1931 to 1932, Dreiser led members of the National Committee for the Defense of Political Prisoners (NCDPP) to Kentucky, where they took testimony from coal miners on the pattern of violence by coal operators against the miners and unions (Harlan County War). Dreiser joined the Communist Party a few months before he died in 1945 of a heart attack in Hollywood.

In 2000, the building was converted into W New York Union Square Hotel by architect David Rockwell, and coffered ceilings, mosaic floors and vaulted marble hallways were restored for the hotel. A grand mahogany and limestone staircase was added to the lobby—a Rockwell signature—along with greenery and a street-side, living room–styled lobby area for hanging out.

Across the street at 100 East Seventeenth Street, the final headquarters of Tammany Hall opened in 1928 under Mayor Jimmy Walker (1881–1946). The three-and-a-half-story building is a New York City landmark designed by the architects Thompson, Holes & Converse and Charles B. Meyers using oversized red brick (Harvard Brik) in a Neo-Georgian (some call it Federal) style. There is the seal of the Tammany Society, sculptural reliefs of Chief Tammany and Christopher Columbus and a Revolutionary War liberty cap, all on the East Seventeenth Street façade. There may be some sort of hidden message in the fact that these same architects who designed Tammany Hall also designed the psychiatric wing of Bellevue Hospital.

Tammany Hall was a political organization founded in 1788 as the Society of St. Tammany or Columbian Order in response to the city's more exclusive clubs (such as the Society of Cincinnati, in which one had to be the firstborn male child of an officer in the Continental army to be a member). Initially, most of the members were craftsmen. The society took the name of a legendary Delaware Indian chief and used pseudo-Indian insignia and titles (braves, sachems etc.). Early on, the group supported Aaron Burr, Martin Van Buren and progressive policies (such as universal male suffrage, a lien law to protect craftsmen and the abolition of debtors prison).

The society expanded its political base by helping immigrants to survive, find work and quickly gain citizenship, but Tammany was not being held accountable and became completely riddled with corruption from the top to the bottom. But still Tammany was more than a temple of political corruption because it opposed anti-Catholic and nativist movements of the era and was strong in its defense of voting rights for all citizens, especially poor immigrants. Tammany traded jobs for votes, and it got mixed in with corruption but still provided work for immigrant labor building the Brooklyn Bridge, Central Park, public schools and the elevated trains and the subways, along with paving the streets. Tammany gained loyalties that lasted for generations. But Tammany's luck changed in 1932 with the (Samuel) Seabury Commission, headed by Governor Franklin D. Roosevelt. This commission led to Mayor Jimmy Walker's resignation in 1932 and, in 1934, to the election of Fiorello La Guardia (1882–1947), a strong reform mayor who reigned for twelve years and fought Tammany on every front. Out of power and unable to meet mortgage payments in 1945, Tammany sold its headquarters on East Seventeenth Street to Local 91 of the International Ladies Garment Workers Union (ILGWU). Tammany Hall had virtually ceased to exist, although some politicians bred in the organization continued to flourish into the 1950s and beyond. Fiorello La Guardia was a Republican mayor from 1934 to 1945. Jimmy Walker was a Democrat and mayor from 1926 to 1932.

Chapter 11

INTRODUCTION AND BOUNDARIES OF UNION SQUARE PARK

UNION SQUARE PARK'S ENVIRONS

S tanding at the corner of East Seventeenth Street and Park Avenue
South and Broadway, we have a view of Union Square bounded by East
Seventeenth Street, East Fourteenth Street, Union Square East and Union
Square West. This is a national landmark historic district. It is a bit strange that
the history of Union Square is, in most ways, opposite to that of Gramercy
Park, not only in its history but also in how both neighborhoods exist today.
Gramercy Park, from its inception, was and is a well-to-do, quiet residential
neighborhood with a sedate private park, whereas Union Square is a robust
retail, commercial and residential neighborhood that is busting at the seams
with activity, both inside the park and in the surrounding neighborhood.
Both were developed by Samuel Ruggles as residential squares and were
part of what were referred to as Manhattan's Four Squares. Actually, of
Manhattan's Four Squares, Union Square was the earliest to be developed.
Samuel Ruggles lived here on Union Square South (East Fourteenth Street).

There were a number of factors or events that facilitated diverging
development in the two residential squares. The theater district traveled
up Broadway, following wealthy New Yorkers, and broke through the
Union Square neighborhood on its way to Herald Square before settling
in Times Square at the turn of the twentieth century. Right behind and/or
along with the theater district came Fashion Row (now called Ladies Mile
Historic District), consisting of upscale department stores catering to the
nineteenth-century carriage trade. Then came the Fourteenth Street subway
station at Union Square in 1904. Along with the theater district and Fashion

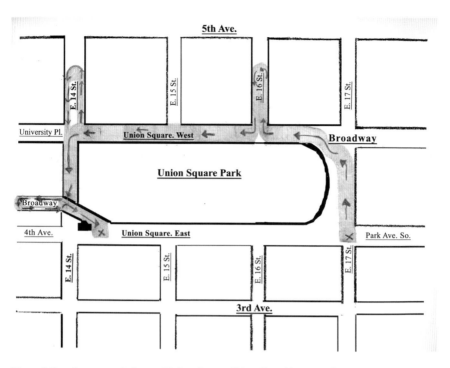

Map of East Seventeenth Street, Union Square West, East Sixteenth Street, East Fourteenth Street to Union Square South.

Row's invasion and subsequent movement northward came a variety of retail stores, restaurants, taverns, music halls (vaudeville and burlesque), hotels, office buildings and the conversion of single family dwellings to multifamily dwellings. All this impacted Union Square while bypassing Gramercy Park, giving rise to two distinctly different neighborhoods.

Union Square Park was laid out in 1830 and opened in 1839 as a public park with an iron fence, a gate that was locked at sundown and keys only for residents in the immediate vicinity. Gaslights were installed in the 1840s, and the residential neighborhood was already changing with the invasion of hotels in the 1850s and other commercial activities in the 1860s. The fence was removed in the 1870s when the park was remodeled by Frederick Law Olmsted and Calvert Vaux (Greensward, Central Park) to accommodate large gatherings. From the early 1860s to the 1880s, out-of-work (sometimes desperate) actors congregated at the south end of the park near the equestrian statue of George Washington—an area that was nicknamed the "slave market"—because theater managers and agents would come to hire performers for upcoming shows. Actors would practice their soliloquies in the park. In the 1880s, they were joined by political orators and union speech makers, and the area became known as Speakers Corner and a working-class meeting place.

As the manufacturing district developed in and around the neighborhood, many different elements sort of blended. During the turn of the twentieth century, upscale department stores were being replaced by discount emporiums like S. Klein and others. Union Square was a civic meeting place for the city's working class, union activists and immigrants and home to the American Communist Party national headquarters and the radical Yiddish newspaper *Freiheit*, along with the Amalgamated Clothing and Textile Workers Union. The Amalgamated Bank, America's first labor-owned bank, was located on Fifteenth Street and Union Square West.

Union Square's history includes the 250,000 people who rallied here to support the Union cause on April 20, 1861, and a gigantic rally in Union Square Park for the United States Colored Troops Twentieth Regiment, in which the Union League Club presented the troops with a flag and a parchment scroll inscribed by club members "Mothers, Wives, and Sisters" (with names that included Astor, Beekman, Fish, Jay and Van Rensselaer). From the park, the troops paraded down Broadway to a Canal Street dock and boarded a steamer to New Orleans and a war zone. In all, over four thousand black New Yorkers fought in the Civil War. Black troops (the U.S. Colored Troops Twentieth Regiment, Twenty-sixth Regiment and the Thirty-first Regiment) were trained on Riker's and Hart Islands and financed by the Union League Club.

On September 5, 1882, twenty-five thousand people marched to Union Square Park from City Hall in the first Labor Day Parade and the tradition continued on for decades. On April 11, 1911, there was a funeral parade at Union Square Park for the unidentified bodies from the Triangle Shirtwaist fire. On August 9, 1927, about fifteen thousand people held a rally and protest in Union Square Park against the executions of Ferdinando Nicola Sacco and Bartolomeo Vanzetti. From the mid-1880s until after World War II, the IWW and other radical groups, along with unions, sponsored any number of May Day rallies and parades at the park. As you can see, most of the traditions and history of Union Square are decidedly different from that of Gramercy Park, only a few blocks away.

But this history is not the reason for the park's name. It was in 1811 that the New York State legislature authorized the Commissioner's Plan, which organized the city's streets into a grid that had several roads—including Bloomingdale Street (Broadway), the Old Bowery Road (Fourth Avenue)

Anarchist May Day crowd in Union Square, 1913. *Courtesy of the Library of Congress.*

and the Union Post Road—all crossing Fourteenth Street at or near the same juncture (a union) and formed sort of an isosceles triangle, which was called the Forks and later named Union Place. The Forks inadvertently created a commons (the land was formerly a potters field) partly covered with rude shanties. In the early 1830s, when Samuel Ruggles began Union Place's development, he configured it into an oval shape and, by 1840, named the residential development Belgravia in Manhattan (Belgravia is a wealthy residential district in central London, England). The land in the development's center was donated (for five dollars) to the city in 1833, and in return, the city agreed to create and maintain a public park, which quickly was surrounded by the mansions of well-to-do New Yorkers, including Ruggles himself at 24 Union Square South (Fourteenth Street). The park soon became known as Union Square.

On the northwest corner of East Seventeenth Street at 200 Park Avenue South is the Everett Building, a small steel-frame skyscraper that opened in 1908. Its architect, Goldwin Starrett & Van Vleck (Goldwin Starrett worked four years in the Chicago offices of Daniel Burnham), used a functionalist design, fostered by Louis Sullivan's Chicago School of Skyscraper Architecture, for the façade. It is a New York City landmark example of the development of a functional, fireproof skyscraper, with a façade styled as a grid that denotes the Chicago school's major precept: to express the building's metal frame on its façade. With simple classical details, its large windows and open floor space, it represents a typical turn-of-the-twentieth-century transitional skyscraper with "architectural decency," as described by A.C. David in the *Architectural Record* of 1910. The ground floor is used for retail space, and there are offices above. There is a vault in the basement that was used by a branch of Chase bank but is now occupied by a clothing store.

During the last half of the nineteenth century, this was the site of the popular Everett Hotel, used by entertainers. Samuel Tilden, former governor of New York and the Democratic candidate for president of the United States, had a party thrown for himself here on November 7, 1876. Tilden won the popular vote by over 250,000 votes, but the electoral college gave the election to Rutherford Hayes.

If we walk west to 33 Union Square North (East Seventeenth Street), we come to the Century Building, which opened in 1881. It is a New York City and a national landmark designed by William Schickel in a Queen Anne style with seventeenth- and eighteenth-century motifs molded in terra cotta, such as its Queen Anne trademark sunflowers plus tall oriel windows, a gambrel roof and prominent chimneys. The building was designed and built as the Century Magazine Headquarters and is now a Barnes & Noble Bookstore.

No. 33 Union Square North, now a Barnes & Noble, formerly the Century Building.

View northward from Union Square North and East Seventeenth Street up Broadway in 1892. *Courtesy of the Library of Congress.*

Century Magazine's more popular publications were the *Century* magazine and the *St. Nicholas* magazine. As we walk to the corner of East Seventeenth Street and look north on Broadway, we can picture how it appeared in 1892, with horse-pulled trollies, carriages and carts crowding the street.

We walk past 35 Union Square West, the site of a Neo-Grec style building that housed G. Schirmer Music Publishers. A company founded in America by a German immigrant in 1861, it published classical music with its own printing and engraving plant. The publisher established Schirmer's Library of Musical Classics, and in 1915, Schirmer and musicologist Oscar Sonneck founded the *Musical Quarterly*, the oldest academic journal on music in the United States.

Walking on to 33 Union Square West, the Decker Building—sometimes referred to as the Union Building—opened in 1893. It is a New York City and a national landmark example of the Moorish style, with Venetian Gothic touches (such as its palazzo-style balconies and motifs on top) along with Art Nouveau (framing of the second-story windows) and classical designs at the top. The naturalistic terra-cotta plant motifs decorate the building's enframements

The west side of Union Square at East Sixteenth Street and the Decker Building in 1894. *Courtesy of the Library of Congress.*

and its intradoses (the space inside of the curves of an arch). The opulence of the façade's design is increased by its limestone, corner quoins on the shaft and its alfiz (the rectangular molding framing the Moorish arch), along with the design effect of its loggia columns. The building was designed by the radical anarchist architect John Edelman working out of the offices of John Zucker for the Decker Brothers Piano Company, founded in 1856.

Islamic and Moorish motifs were part of a long-lived exotic movement in design prompted by the trade and exploration of the eighteenth and nineteenth centuries. Moorish details are often used to suggest an escape from the mundane, and the idea of pleasure from pianos may have inspired Edelman to use the style.

Andy Warhol (1928–1987) had his sixth-floor Factory here from 1968 to 1973. It was in June 1968 on the sixth floor of this building that he was shot in the stomach by Valerie Solanas, a young woman who was part of his entourage and disappointed because he refused to produce her screenplay. Warhol survived, but security became very tight and the mood was tense. Directorial duties were taken over by Paul Morrissey, who went on to do more commercial films. *Flesh* (1968), *Trash* (1970) and *Heat* (1972) were all produced here.

Andy Warhol was born Pittsburgh, graduated Carnegie Institute and worked as a freelance commercial artist, painter and filmmaker. He died in 1987 after a gall bladder removal operation at New York Hospital. He made experimental films, such as *Sleep* (1963), which depicts John Giorno sleeping five hours and twenty minutes, and *Chelsea Girls* (1966), considered controversial for its eroticism. Warhol made the famous remark that in the future, everyone would be famous for fifteen minutes.

Valerie Solanas (1936–1988) ended up in a mental hospital and later moved to San Francisco, California, where she died of pneumonia. She was an angry feminist who founded the Society for Cutting Up Men (SCUM).

Next door, at 34 Union Square West (19–23 East Sixteenth Street), the Bank of the Metropolis opened 1903. It is a New York City and a national landmark designed as a tower with a limestone Neo-Renaissance façade that features classical elements such as an imposing, two-story bowed portico with monumental polished granite columns; lions' heads; consoles; and foliate spandrels that were associated with American bank architecture of the day and meant to inspire authority. The bank was designed by architect Bruce Price, who lived at 12 West Tenth Street with his family. His daughter grew up to be Emily Post, the "First Lady of American Etiquette."

Union Square, 1905, with the Bank of the Metropolis in the background (with the American flag on top). *Courtesy of the Library of Congress.*

The Bank of the Metropolis had powerful neighborhood businessmen on its board of directors, such as decorator/glassmaker Louis Comfort Tiffany and publisher Charles Scribner, and their presence helped to attract support from other local merchants. In 1918, the Bank of the Metropolis was absorbed by the Bank of Manhattan, and in 1955, the Bank of Manhattan Co. merged with Chase Manhattan.

We will now take a half block detour from the park's perimeter and walk west to 16 East Sixteenth Street. Built as the Margaret Louise Home (YWCA) Lodging House in 1890, it is now the Sidney Hillman Health Center. Upstairs is the New York City Free Clinic, run by NYU. The Institute for Urban Family Health also operates two free clinics for the uninsured at this location. The clinics opened in March 2002 with medical students supervised at all times by senior physicians. The free clinics are open on Saturday mornings, offering medical care, health education and social work services for adults. Social workers enroll children in Child Health Plus (CHIP) and try to obtain insurance for adults.

117

Hansom cab and driver in Union Square, 1896. *Staten Island Historical Society Collection.*

The original architect was Robert Henderson Robertson (1849–1919), who designed the building with rock-faced brownstone in a Romanesque Revival style that includes a nice colonnade and gargoyles on top. Mrs. Margaret Vanderbilt Shepard (Cornelius Vanderbilt's eldest daughter) was a major benefactor here.

Sidney Hillman (1887–1946), a founder and president (1914–46) of the garment workers' union (Amalgamated Clothing Workers of America, now UNITE!), also was a founder of the Committee of Industrial Organization (CIO) and a political ally of Franklin D. Roosevelt.

For the next stop, we return to the park's perimeter and pass the southwest corner of East Fifteenth Street and Union Square West. This was the site for which architect John Kellum designed the cast-iron Tiffany & Co. Store, modeling it after a Venetian palace. Tiffany & Co. was here from 1870 to 1906. The firm moved to Fifth Avenue in Murray Hill and then to its present location at Fifth Avenue and East Fifty-seventh Street.

In 1837, Charles Lewis Tiffany (1812–1902) and John B. Young founded Tiffany, Young and Ellis in Lower Manhattan as a "stationery and fancy goods emporium," selling a variety of stationery items. Charles Tiffany took over in 1853, changing the name to Tiffany & Company and the firm's specialty to jewelry. Tiffany's son was Lewis Comfort Tiffany (1848–1933), an American artist and designer who worked in the decorative arts and is closely associated with Art Nouveau and remembered for his stained-glass windows, lamps, glass mosaics, blown glass, ceramics, jewelry and more. Tiffany was closely affiliated with other artists such as Lockwood de Forest, Candace Wheeler and Samuel Colman, among others.

By 1952, the building was owned by Amalgamated Bank. The original façade was stripped and covered with white brick, which was unchanged until 2006, when the building was sold and the original six-story façade was dismantled. Its original arches were restored and wrapped behind a façade of glass and black-anodized aluminum and then topped by six added stories to create thirty-six glass condominiums. Blending historic and contemporary elements, they were designed by Eran Chen (ODA-Architecture).

We are now looking at the northwest corner of East Fourteenth Street at 1–3 Union Square West. The Lincoln Building opened in 1890. It is a New York City and a national landmark designed by Robert H. Robertson, and it represents the very early transitional stage of skyscraper construction because it has a metal frame inside the masonry load-bearing walls (as it was a concern that the building would fall with only a steel frame to support it). Within a decade, it was realized the steel frame was stronger and completely replaced the masonry load-bearing walls in skyscrapers, the steel frame being the essential criteria of a true skyscraper. The building was designed with a Romanesque Revival, Indiana limestone, brick and granite façade. The fenestration—the horizontal pattern of the façade's windows—emphasize the traditional massiveness of its masonry walls, and the façade's arcades stress its metal, skeletal frame.

At the top are forty little windows and paired columns over a granite cornice with griffins. The medieval Romanesque ornamented façade includes stone carvings drawn from Byzantine, Norman and Celtic designs including Acanthus scrolls and Byzantine capitals and heads. On the corner near the seventh floor is one large, winged, grotesque griffin (or gargoyle) with a distorted face and legs that are almost human. Initially, it served as a flagpole. The sixth floor of this building houses the remodeled offices of the *New Republic* magazine.

If we walk about half a block west on East Fourteenth Street (toward Fifth Avenue), we will pass the defunct address 11 East Fourteenth Street, the site of the brownstone Victorian Cunard mansion that was converted in 1906 into the second headquarters for Biograph Studios (American Mutoscope and Biograph Company). Biograph Studios was one of the earliest studios to

Lincoln Building, 1–3 Union Square West.

produce silent movies and became famous with such silent film stars as Mary Pickford, Lillian and Dorothy Gish, Lionel Barrymore and Max Sennett. D.W. Griffith directed his first movie, *The Adventures of Dolly*, here in 1908. In 1911, Griffith purchased seven scripts from Harriet Quimby (1875–1912) and made them into silent movies, making her the first successful female screenwriter in America. Harriet was also the first licensed female pilot in America. On April 16, 1912, she became the first female pilot to fly her plane across the English Channel. Harriet was living and working in Manhattan from 1903 to 1912. She stayed at the Victoria Hotel on Broadway and East Twenty-seventh Street and was a staff writer for *Leslie's Illustrated Weekly*. Her face is shown on a fifty-cent airmail stamp. Harriet was a beautiful, courageous woman whose pioneering accomplishments pointed the way for other female pilots, such as Amelia Earhart.

As we walk back east on East Fourteenth Street to 24 Union Place, we are passing the site of Samuel Ruggles's home. Ruggles developed both Gramercy Park and Union Square Park as two of Manhattan's Four Squares (see chapter 1).

As we continue our walk, we are passing the site of 46–48 East Fourteenth Street (between University Place and Broadway), where in 1903, Adolph Zukor (1873–1976) opened Automatic Vaudeville, a penny arcade offering entertainment that included everything from fortunetelling to burlesque and

Harriet Quimby in the cockpit of her plane in 1911. *Courtesy of the Library of Congress.*

vaudeville peep shows with titles like "My Cosey Corner Girl," "Hannah, Won't You Open That Door," "An Affair of Honor" and "South African Warriors." The penny arcades catered to both men and women, but silent films and then talkies gradually replaced the arcades. Adolph Zukor was a Hungarian immigrant who went on to be a founder of Paramount Pictures.

If we take a short detour, we come to the Roosevelt Building, 839–41 Broadway at the northwest corner of East Thirteenth Street, named for Cornelius Roosevelt (Theodore Roosevelt's grandfather), who had a mansion near the site. The building's rooftop was the original site for Biograph Studios from 1896 to 1906, before it moved.

If we continue to walk east on East Fourteenth Street and look at the top of the buildings between Broadway and Fourth Avenue, we'll see "Metronome," a large public art installation commissioned at a cost of $42 million by Related Companies (developers) with the involvement of the Public Art Fund and the Municipal Art Society. It began in February 1999, and the dedication was on October 26, 1999. The installation was created by contemporary American artists Kristin Jones (b. 1956) and Andrew Ginzel (b. 1954). The artwork is made up of several sections, including "Infinity," a circular hole that emits steam at noon and midnight, and "Passage," a large

LED digital reverse clock with changing, five-foot-high orange numbers that are read from the center. From the center reading to the left displays the hours, minutes and seconds that remain in the day, and reading to the right displays the hours, minutes and seconds that have passed in the day. It is a clock but a very confusing clock, indeed. "Relic" is a large replica of the right hand of George Washington from the statue across Fourteenth Street. And the phases of the moon are mirrored by a five-foot rotating gold sphere. This multimedia sculpture is made up of brick, concrete, steel, aluminum, gold leaf, incandescent light, steam and sound.

By the 1870s, Union Square was well on its way to becoming the entertainment capital of the country, and by 1890, the theater district had moved to Herald Square. The building at 58 East Fourteenth Street was the site of the Union Square Theater, located between Fourth Avenue and Broadway. From 1871 to 1888, it was part of the Union Place Hotel (Morton Hotel). Rebuilt in 1889, it was known as the Drawing Room Theater of America until 1893, when it was purchased by B.F. Keith. Beginning in 1871, the theater offered comedy, ballet, pantomime and legitimate plays, and in 1908, it converted over to silent films and later to talkies (movies). As a movie house, it offered racy movies and sex lectures. In 1932, it changed to all Soviet films and offered membership to the Communist Party. This lasted until 1936, when the theater closed, the ground floor was divided up for stores and the part of the building not being used was walled off. The building was demolished in 1995, destroying remnants of a small part of the Rialto's history on Union Square.

If we walk east to the southeast corner of Fourth Avenue and East Fourteenth Street, we will be at the site where a beautiful Victorian building—that could easily have served as a symbol of the German American contribution to Manhattan's growth and diversity—was replaced in 1962 by a nondescript brick apartment building. Between 1845 and 1855, a wave of over 800,000 Germans (including both impoverished workers and successful businessmen) migrated to New York. By 1872, the German Savings Bank opened on this corner with German-speaking tellers. It was a five-story building designed by Henry Fernback and Edward H. Kendall with a chamfered corner and French Second Empire details. During World War I, the bank changed its name to the Central Savings Bank of the City of New York. In 1927, the building's lower floors became a local branch office when the bank's executive offices moved to a new building at West Seventy-third Street and Broadway, and in the 1940s, the upper floors were rented to the New York County Committee of the Communist Party.

A run on the German Savings Bank on August 3, 1914. *Courtesy of the Library of Congress.*

From here we walk north to Zeckendorf Towers (opened 1987), one square block from East Fourteenth Street to East Fifteenth Street and Union Square East to Irving Place. It is a modern, mixed-use luxury condominium complex with four pyramidal crowned towers over a massive commercial base designed by Davis Brody & Assoc. This was the site of a group of small nineteenth-century buildings that combined in 1921 to become the home of S. Klein's on the Square, one of the original discount department stores featuring bargains and occasional high style. Its large neon sign became well known on Union Square, and its name, "Klein's on the Square," had a double meaning—the store offered a square deal and was located on Union Square East. Also on a small part of Zeckendorf Towers' site, at the southeast corner of East Fifteenth Street and Union Square East, was where the Union Square Hotel (demolished in 1986) opened in 1871.

On October 29, 1897, Henry George (1839–1897) died in the hotel from a heart attack. He was an influential writer, politician and political economist and a strong proponent of "Single-Tax" (land value tax and the value capture of land and natural resource rents). He inspired several reform movements of the Progressive Era and the economic philosophy referred to as Georgism. Its main idea is that people own value they create but that common resources and the value of land belongs equally to all humanity. His book *Progress and Poverty* (1879) sold millions of copies and is a treatise on inequality describing how the land value tax can solve problems created by the cyclic nature of industrialized economies. George's popularity is now forgotten, but his funeral held in New York City's Grand Central Palace exhibition hall (on Lexington Avenue between East Forty-third Street and East Forty-fourth Street) was attended by over 100,000 people.

Across the street is 20 Union Square East. It opened as the Union Square Bank in 1907 and is a New York City landmark designed with bold academic classicism by architect Henry Bacon (1866–1924). The handsome white granite building with a Corinthian temple front features four colossal fluted Corinthian columns supporting an entablature and a parapet. There are matching pilasters on the East Fifteenth Street façade. The bank had the monumental style of a Greek or Roman temple, and the interior banking room was fitted with marble, bronze and stained-glass skylights that are sixty feet above the floor. Henry Bacon was a prolific Beaux Arts architect best remembered for the Lincoln Memorial in Washington, D.C. In 1923, Bacon became the sixth recipient of the American Institute of Architects (AIA) Gold Medal presented to him by President Warren G. Harding.

In 1968, the bank changed to the United Mutual Savings Bank and in 1982 was acquired by the American Savings Bank. In 1992, it closed for good (after a series of bad real estate loans), and the impressive building is now used by the Daryl Roth Theater.

We will cross Union Square East at East Fifteenth Street and look into the park.

Chapter 12

UNION SQUARE PARK, MEMORIALS AND STATUES

Marquis de Lafayette to Abraham Lincoln

O n the east side of Union Square Park between East Fifteenth and East Sixteenth Streets is a bronze, larger-than-life statue of Marquis de Lafayette created in 1873 and dedicated in 1876. It is on a granite pedestal by H.W. DeStuckle. Sculptor Frederic Auguste Bartholdi (1834–1904) intended to create a work that plainly portrays the act of arrival and the passion of the hero. Lafayette is standing on ship's prow, pledging his heart and sword to the American Revolution. Actually, at first glance, you might think of an actor on stage in a historical melodrama. When Lafayette arrived in America with soldiers, supplies and his own fortune, he was given a congressional commission as a major general in the Continental army. His success in aiding the revolutionaries helped persuade France to send supplies and Rochambeau's expeditionary force, which aided Washington in his decisive victory at Yorktown. Lafayette became a hero and a legend, and in 1824, President Monroe invited Lafayette to revisit and tour the United States. His year-long tour began with a historic visit to New York City, which was marked by Samuel B. Morse's famous painting of the older Lafayette that is still hanging in city hall to this day.

The statue is a gift from the French government in recognition of aid given by New Yorkers to Parisians during the Franco-Prussian War (July 1870 to May 1871). The French residents in New York City paid for the pedestal.

Frederic Auguste Bartholdi was a French sculptor best known for creating the Statue of Liberty in France. Supposedly Bartholdi modeled the face on the statue after his mother. In 1886, the statue was given to the

Union Square Park map.

United States and to all people who aspire to liberty as a gift from the French and American people. Bartholdi has over a dozen major works in France and America. In New York City, he has three works still on public display: the Statue of Liberty, *Marquis de Lafayette* and *Lafayette and Washington*, a replica in Morningside Park.

Near the corner of East Fifteenth Street and Union Square East is a subway entrance to the Fourteenth Street–Union Square New York City Subway station complex (a national landmark) that exists under Union Square Park. It is shared by the IRT Lexington Avenue Line, the BMT Broadway Line and the BMT Canarsie Line (4, 5, 6, L, N, Q and R trains). Before 1940, there were three separate subway lines that had separate stations at Union Square. The subways were unified in 1940, and the three stations here under Union Square were combined, sharing street entrances, a mezzanine and unified signage.

The IRT Lexington Avenue Line (4, 5 and 6 trains) was the earliest subway line at Union Square. It opened in 1904 and was part of the city's first subway system that ran from city hall to Forty-second Street and Park

Avenue (Grand Central Station) and then across Forty-second Street to Broadway (Times Square) and up the west side on Broadway to 145th Street. The IRT was soon followed by BMT Broadway Line, opened in 1917, and the BMT Canarsie Line, opened in 1921.

Next we walk back to East Fourteenth Street and Broadway. Inside Union Square Park between Broadway and University Place, facing East Fourteenth Street, is the bronze, fourteen-foot-high equestrian statue of George Washington created in 1855 and dedicated on July 4, 1856. The sculptor was Henry Kirke Brown (1814–1886), along with his assistant, John Quincy Adams Ward. The statue is on a granite pedestal designed by Richard Upjohn, and it is part of the collection of the City of New York. It was paid for by public subscription. The contributors were wealthy merchants who lived in the fashionable Union Square neighborhood, and they stipulated the equestrian format and the location. Brown chose to depict the moment on November 25, 1783, when Washington officially reclaimed the city from the British. He came down Broadway with his troops from the Van Cortlandt house, stopping where Broadway meets Fourteenth Street, and made his proclamation. The statue was erected on this spot on a small fenced-in plot in the middle of the street. Several decades later, it was moved into Union Square Park because of a number of vehicular accidents.

George Washington statue on Union Square Park North near East Fourteenth Street.

This was New York City's first major outdoor bronze. It is considered both dignified and vigorous and was an example of Brown's belief that the American heritage should be celebrated by artists using simple and direct naturalism. Brown initiated a formula for America's statuary—utilizing a quiet grandeur and a harmony with classical composition and realistic detail—that lasted twenty-five years. Brown has depicted Washington erect in his saddle with his arm outstretched and his palm faced downward. This gesture and the overall composition evoke the famous classical equestrian statue of Marcus Aurelius by Michelangelo on Capitoline Hill in Rome, so it seems Brown suggests that Washington deserves to be compared to the Roman emperor. This was the second equestrian statue to be cast in the United States (most were cast abroad). The first was Clark Mills's Andrew Jackson opposite the White House in Washington, D.C.

Brown studied Washington's uniform, which was preserved in Washington, D.C., and his design was also guided by Jean-Antoine Houdon's (1741–1828) likeness of Washington.

We are walking to the southwest corner of the park at East Fourteenth Street and Union Square West, where there is a small pedestrian triangle with a larger-than-life bronze statue of Mohandas Gandhi, dedicated on October 2, 1986. The sculptor is Kantilal B. Patel (born 1925). The statue is on a granite pedestal and is part of the collection of the City of New York. It was commissioned by the Gandhi Memorial International Foundation.

An advocate of nonviolent protest, Mohandas Gandhi (1869–1948), aka Mahatma (Great Soul) Gandhi, is depicted here with his walking stick and wearing a dhoti, a reference to Hindu asceticism. The simple homespun garment also reminds us of his efforts to revive Indian home industries, such as the spinning of yarn. Gandhi was one of this century's extraordinary political leaders. An Indian nationalist, he dedicated his life to India's struggle for independence from the British, and he advocated passive noncooperation, initiating boycotts and personal fasts. Union Square Park has a long tradition of protest, and Gandhi joins the American patriots Lincoln, Washington and Lafayette.

At the southwest corner of the park was the well-known location of "Dead Man's Curve," which began at the intersection of Broadway and East Fourteenth Street when the cable cars made a left turn to Union Square West and continued northward. Cable cars were pulled by cables that ran under Broadway, and they were pulled by a huge steam engine that turned twenty-six-foot-diameter wheels. The whole apparatus was located in the basement of the Cable Building, which is still standing at the northwest

Gandhi statue at Union Square West and East Fourteenth Street. *Original watercolor by Ann Woodward.*

corner of Broadway and Houston Streets, and the name Cable Building is still carved over its Broadway entrance, although everything else is but a memory. From the early 1890s, Union Square was an incredible death trap and notorious for its Dead Man's Curve. You see, the cables ran underground at a constant, optimal speed for going in a straight line. When the cars would get to the curve, the conductors would shout for everyone to hang on as they zipped and rocketed through the curve. Unsuspecting riders were tossed about, sometimes out onto the cobblestones, and on the street, busy pedestrians were being mutilated and slaughtered by the speeding cable cars. Between 1929 and 1940, Union Square was torn up to make way for the massive underground transportation hub that combined three underground

Union Square, Dead Man's Curve, 1908. *Courtesy of the Library of Congress.*

subway stations, and Dead Man's Curve disappeared completely from the new Union Square. The statue of Abraham Lincoln stood at one corner of Dead Man's Curve (where the statue of Gandhi now stands) and must have witnessed much of the bloodshed, and the Lincoln Building just across the street may have been named because of the statue. Lincoln's statue was moved deeper inside the northern section of the park in the 1930s during the park's reconstruction.

And now we proceed to an alcove with a fountain right off Union Park West inside the park between East Fifteenth and East Sixteenth Streets. The purpose of the fountain was threefold: to increase the physical comfort of New Yorkers, to inspire religion and charity to New Yorkers and to encourage a healthy appreciation of art. The Union Square Drinking Fountain, also known as the James Fountain, was dedicated on October 25, 1881. It is a bronze, larger-than-life sculpture on a pink granite (quarried in Sweden) stepped, octagonal pedestal, and the sculptor was Adolph von Donndorf (1835–1916). The fountain is part of the collection of the City of New York and was a gift of Daniel Willis James (1832–1907), who came up with the idea for the fountain while on a trip to Germany with Theodore Roosevelt (businessman and philanthropist at the time). For the Union Square Drinking Fountain, Donndorf used his family as models for the tableau. The primary figure is a mother holding an infant and a water pitcher, with a small boy at her side. There are bronze lion heads that serve as water spouts on four sides, along with sculptural flourishes depicting butterflies, salamanders and figures with biblical associations. When the fountain was first created, there were metal cups chained to it, permitting people to drink the water.

When the Croton Reservoir aqueduct was completed in 1842, it supplied New York City with a consistent supply of fresh water, so the city no longer needed to use its (often contaminated) well water. This public health advancement was celebrated by drinking fountains built in City Hall Park, Central Park and Union Square Park, along with other outdoor decorative drinking fountains that were created throughout the city for man and beast.

And from here, just walk toward the center of the park to the Independence Flagstaff (Charles F. Murphy Memorial). It was cast in 1926 and dedicated on July 4, 1930. It is part of the collection of the City of New York and was donated by the Tammany Society. The architects were Perry Coke Smith and Charles B. Meyers, and the sculptor was Anthony de Francisci (1887–1964).

Francisci created the drum bas-reliefs for the huge flagpole capped by a gilded sunburst on top. The intricate bas-reliefs display a procession of allegorical figures that start from the rear and show the effects of liberty and democracy as a march of progress in the arts, crafts and sciences, and the figures move toward a tablet on the front that contains the text from the Declaration of Independence.

The flagstaff commemorates both the 150th anniversary of the signing of the Declaration of Independence and the memory of Tammany boss Charles F. Murphy. When this flagstaff was installed in 1930, it replaced an earlier one that had been dedicated to Murphy. Public sentiment at the time against the infamously corrupt Tammany political machine prevented supporters from putting up a statue to honor Murphy. Over the years, the flagstaff has been extensively restored.

Sculptor Francisci immigrated to the United States from Italy in 1905 and became a citizen in 1913. He lived and studied in New York City under fine coin designers and worked as an academician at the National Academy of Design, besides having his own commissions. Francisci's most notable work was the Peace Dollar in 1921. His other works included the National Guard Bureau insignia, the 1920 Maine Centennial commemorative half dollar, a Lincoln medal for the Hall of Fame for Great Americans in New York and an inaugural medal for the 1964–65 New York's World Fair.

Abraham Lincoln statue in the center of Union Square Park at East Sixteenth Street.

At the north end of the park, about halfway between Union Square East and Union Square West, is the last stop on the walking tour, the statue of Abraham Lincoln, cast in 1870 and dedicated on September 16, 1870. It's a bronze eight-foot figure with an integral plinth on a granite pedestal created by sculptor Henry Kirke Brown (1814–1886) and donated by public subscription sponsored by the Union League Club. This is one of three statues of Abraham Lincoln in the collection of the City of New York.

Abraham Lincoln (1809–1865), the sixteenth president of the United States, was born in a Kentucky log cabin. He was mostly self-educated and in 1821 settled in New Salem, Illinois, where he studied law and worked as a storekeeper, surveyor and postmaster. Lincoln won four elections to the state legislature and from 1847 to 1849 was elected to Congress on the Whig ticket for one term. He returned to his legal practice until the repeal of the Missouri Compromise (which threatened to spread slavery to the west) in 1854 pulled him back into politics. In 1856 and 1858, Lincoln lost two bids for the United State Senate, but the seven debates with his Democratic opponent, Stephen A. Douglas, gained him national recognition.

Lincoln visited New York City in 1860 and made his famous "right makes might" speech at Cooper Union. He was elected president on the Republican ticket. By April 1861, eleven southern states seceded from the Union, joined the Confederacy and fired on Fort Sumter, plunging us into the Civil War. In 1863, Lincoln issued the Emancipation Proclamation, freeing the slaves, and delivered the Gettysburg Address, fulfilling his role as a skillful orator and a thoughtful leader. He was reelected president in 1864.

Lincoln was assassinated by John Wilkes Booth at Ford's Theater in Washington, D.C., on April 15, 1865, five days after Confederate general Robert E. Lee surrendered. His funeral cortege traveled to cities throughout the United States, and his body lay in state at city hall in Manhattan on April 24. Lincoln is buried at Oak Ridge Cemetery in Springfield, Illinois.

Even though Henry Kirke Brown did travel to Italy to study early on, he became part of a group of sculptors attempting to establish a true American sculptural idiom. Brown combines a classically styled pose with a perceptive naturalism, fusing realistic detail with an idealistic stance. Brown created a similar portrait of Lincoln in Prospect Park, and Henry Kirke Bush-Brown, his nephew and pupil, created the bronze bust for Gettysburg's Lincoln Memorial.

Lincoln's statue originally stood at the southwest corner of Union Square at the site of today's Gandhi statue. It probably inspired the name for the Lincoln Building, erected on the adjacent corner across Union Square West. Union Square Park was completely redesigned in 1930 to accommodate new subway construction, and Lincoln's statue was relocated to its present spot in the park's northern section and placed in axial alignment with the Independence Flagpole (1930) and Henry Kirke Brown's striking equestrian statue of George Washington, located at the park's southern plaza. The Abraham Lincoln statue was conserved in 1992.

The stop between the Gramercy Park neighborhood and Union Square is the museum home of Theodore Roosevelt. It is easy to see Roosevelt's presidential legacy of trust busting and conservationism as being sympathetic to some of the views of unionist and radicals who frequented Union Square. President Theodore Roosevelt called his domestic program the Square Deal, and he formed the program on three ideas: the conservation of natural resources, the control of corporations and consumer protection. These ideas were referred to as the "three C's" of Roosevelt's Square Deal, and Roosevelt's purpose was to attack plutocracy and bad trust. His goal was to help the average citizen. As a Progressive Republican, Roosevelt can be viewed as a connecting link between the wealthy residents of Gramercy Park and the working-class activists of Union Square.

The last stop, Abraham Lincoln's statue, can be seen as a symbol for holding together not only people of different classes but also people with different views of humanity. Lincoln saved the union from splitting in two and kept our nation together, despite the stark differences between the North and the South. Lincoln's statue at Union Square reminds us of the tremendous sacrifices made by the people of the United States so that we could remain united as one country, thereby placing the diverging histories and legacies of Gramercy Park and Union Square into a larger more complex context that, on one hand, can symbolize today's divisions in our country as a whole but, on the other hand, reminds us how well the two neighbors exist, cooperate and are a part of the same city.

BIBLIOGRAPHY

Burrows, Edwin G., and Mike Wallace. *Gotham: A History of New York City to 1898*. New York: Oxford University Press, 1999.

Byron, Joseph, with text by Albert K. Baragwanath. *New York Life at the Turn of the Century*. New York: Dover Publications, 1985.

Diamondstein, Barbaralee. *The Landmarks of New York*. Vol. 2. New York: Harry N. Abrams Inc., 1993.

Dodson, Howard, Christopher Moore and Roberta Yancy. *The Black New Yorkers: The Schomburg Illustrated Chronology*. New York: John Wiley & Sons, Inc., 2000.

Dolkhart, Andrew S., and Matthew A. Postal. *Guide to New York City Landmarks*. 4th ed. Edited by Matthew A. Postal. New York City Landmarks Preservation Commission. Hoboken, NJ: John Wiley & Sons, 2009.

Eastman, John. *Who Lived Where: A Biographical Guide to Homes and Museums*. New York: Bonanza Books, 1983.

Ellis, Edward Robb. *The Epic of New York City*. New York: Old Town Books, 1990.

Gale, Margot, and Michele Cohen. *The Art Commission and the Municipal Art Society Guide to Manhattan's Outdoor Sculpture*. New York: Harper Collins Publishers, 1988.

Garney, Andrew. *Gramercy Park: An Illustrated History of a New York Neighborhood*. New York: Balsam Press, Inc., Rutledge Books, 1984.

Holmes, Julia. *100 New Yorkers: A Guide to Illustrious Lives & Locations*. New York: Little Bookroom, 2004.

Jackson, T. Kenneth, ed. *The Encyclopedia of New York City*. 2nd ed. New Haven, CT: Yale University Press, 2010.

King, Moses. *King's Handbook of New York City*. Boston: Moses King, 1892.

Klein, Carole. *Gramercy Park: An American Bloomsbury*. Athens: Ohio University Press, 1992.

Shaver, Peter D. comp. *The National Register of Historic Places in New York State*. Compiled for the Preservation League of New York State. New York: Rizzoli International Publications Inc., 1993.

Smith, Gene E. *American Gothic: The Story of America's Legendary Theatrical Family—Junius, Edwin, and John Wilkes Booth*. New York: Touchstone Book, Simon & Schuster, 1992.

Stern, Robert A.M., Thomas Mellins, and David Fishman. *New York 1880 Architecture and Urbanism in the Gilded Age*. New York: Monacelli Press, 1999.

White, Norval, and Elliot Willensky, with Fran Leadon. *AIA Guide to New York City*. 5th ed. New York: Oxford University Press, 2010.

Wolfe, Gerard R. *New York: A Guide to the Metropolis Walking Tours of Architecture and History*. 2nd ed. New York: McGraw Hill, 1994.

The WPA Guide to New York City: The Federal Writers Project Guide to 1930's New York. Introduction by William Whyte. New York: New Press, 1992.

INDEX

ABOUT THE AUTHORS

Alfred Pommer of New York City Cultural Walking Tours is a self-employed licensed New York City guide. He has been giving private and publicly scheduled neighborhood walking tours for groups or individuals in Manhattan's many diverse neighborhoods for over twenty-five years. During that time, Alfred has been constantly researching and improving each tour. He retired in 1991 after twenty-five years of service with the New York City Parks Department. During that time, he attended college part time, eventually graduating Empire College, SUNY with a bachelor of science degree in labor studies. Alfred has authored three previous guidebooks: *Exploring New York's SoHo*, *Exploring the Original West Village* and *Exploring Manhattan's Murray Hill*, all published by The History Press. He has also had several articles published about the history of various locations, streets and neighborhoods in Manhattan published by *10003 Magazine*.

www.nycwalk.com

Joyce Pommer is an abstract mixed media artist and independent curator. Having owned a gallery in Manhattan for eight years, as director she wrote press releases and artist synopses. Now she has returned to focus on her own painting and is reemerging as Joyce Pommer + Projects. Originally from Boston, Joyce studied at the Academy of Art College in San Francisco, the Art Institute of Boston and the Art Students League in New York City.

She has exhibited in numerous solo and group shows in New York City and across the country, and her works are included in numerous private collections. She maintains a studio in the garment district in Manhattan.

Joyce also works as a nurse consultant for a law firm reviewing medical records and writing case reports. This is her second venture in co-authoring with her husband, Alfred.

www.joycepommer.com